A JOURNEY
OF
UNCONDITIONAL
LOVE

Joe B

What a
Wonderful Life

Pleasure to meet you

Micke

2019

A JOURNEY
OF
UNCONDITIONAL
LOVE

A LOVE STORY BETWEEN A MOTHER AND SON

MICHELE BELL

BALBOA.
PRESS
A DIVISION OF HAY HOUSE

Balboa Press books may be ordered through booksellers or by contacting:

Balboa Press
A Division of Hay House
1663 Liberty Drive
Bloomington, IN 47403
www.balboapress.com
1 (877) 407-4847

Print information available on the last page.

ISBN: 978-1-5043-9453-6 (sc)
ISBN: 978-1-5043-9455-0 (hc)
ISBN: 978-1-5043-9454-3 (e)

Library of Congress Control Number: 2017919759

Balboa Press rev. date: 03/22/2018

"In the transparent, authentic voice that only a mother could possess, Michele Bell opens her heart and soul in *A Journey of Unconditional Love*. This is far more than a parent's account of the heartache and despair associated with the loss of a child to cancer. This is a book about life and legacy. You will be strengthened and inspired by this story. I have personally traveled this same path in my own life and I can say that this is truly a book that not only needs to be read. It needs to be shared."

Matt Patterson
Keynote Speaker / Corporate Trainer – Matt Patterson International
Author – Amazon #1 International Best-Seller – *My Emily*

Michele Bell has created a powerful love story between a mother and son. It's inspiring to go on Michele's journey of the heart as she takes something tragic and creates meaning and beauty. Her compassionate exploration of grief, loss and love helps us to embrace the gift of life. A Journey of Unconditional Love is a soulful journey into heartbreak and coming out the other end with purpose, trust and undying love.

Paul Denniston
Grief Yoga Teacher

They say time heals all wounds. I believe time simply rewards us with the opportunity to play a larger role in a much bigger story. Michele and Nicky's journey is courageous, and I'm sure it will serve it's greater purpose to help many others out there put their stories into a new context...to help us all."

- Michael Bell, renowned American artist and author of DUAL LIVES

Nicky Bell, who I never met has inspired me to become a better person through the reading of this book written by a Mother who loved her son more than she could ever love herself. "A Journey of Unconditional Love" is a must read. Michele is someone who you love as soon as you meet her. Michele Bell is a dear friend and a very loving and caring person. I am honored and blessed to be on life's journey with Michele.

Michele, you are an inspiration to anyone you meet! Thanks for being my friend. And what a Mother to Nicky you will always be!!!

Love and hugs,
Freddie Ganno - Actor

"Michele Bell's memoir about the death of her beloved child, is a true testament to her courage. She faces grief head on and spiritually finds a way to continue helping others in her struggle to make sense of her loss."

Laurie Burrows Grad
Journalist - Huffington Post

A powerful, emotional journey that strengthens, comforts, and inspires - I highly recommend this to all of my patients experiencing grief and loss.

Carlise C. Downie, MSW, LCSW

"Warning, this story may change your life. It will open your heart in unexpected ways."

Donna Cardillo, RN, CSP The Inspiration Nurse and award-winning author of Falling Together: How to Find Balance, Joy, and Meaningful Change When Your Life Seems to be Falling Apart.

I remember the thrill and excitement for my Michele who was on the precipice of the release of her long awaited book. I encourage everyone to support and read the book, there are life lessons for everyone in this book.

A heartfelt true story that will bring tears of joy and happiness. A true lesson of the human condition we all share. How it effects us and how we can continue to live life in the most positive way possible. We are all passing through, this book teaches how to stop and smell the roses, to appreciate the very essence of life for what it is.

Renzo Baronti

After reading " A Journey of Unconditional Love " by my childhood friend Michelle Bell, I find myself inspired as a mother and educator. Her emotional honesty of tragedy, pain and suffering through a mothers loss and sons strength will forever have a lasting impact on my life especially looking back and understanding my own grief after losing my only sister tragically at age 22. A million thanks to Michele

Lainie Damaskos-Christou
National Board Certified World Language Teacher
Niskayuna Central School District. Niskayuna New York
Professor of Greek and Spanish -The College of St. Rose. Albany NY

CONTENTS

"*We are pressed on every side by troubles, but we are not crushed or broken. We are perplexed, but we won't give up and quit. We are hunted down, but God never abandons us. We get knocked down, but we get back up and keep going.*"

— Nicky Bell
June 20, 1987 - December 29, 2005

His faith was authentic as a young man

THE LOSS OF A CHILD

"PARENTS OF CHILD loss learn to become the great deceivers early on. They have to put on a mask because people don't understand—they can't understand—the pain that a bereaved parent wrestles with day and night when a child is gone forever. There are a million tears cried inside the heart every day. There are moments of screaming, begging, and pleading. But others don't see this. Most people tend to avoid feeling empathy. The reason is simple—it hurts. So our wings we carry become the greatest source of strength of all time. If others knew the torment that went on in a parent's heart and mind, they would stand back and wonder how there is any breath left inside of that broken, wounded body. There is simply no greater pain than that of losing a child. There is absolutely nothing to compare."

— Michele Bell, Ph.D.

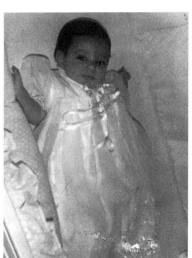

DOES TIME REALLY HEAL ALL WOUNDS?

"THEY SAY TIME heals all wounds. I believe time simply rewards us with the opportunity to play a larger role in a much bigger story, one too large for us to see while we are in the midst of 'living it'. This has often been the case in my life, and it seems also to be the case for Michele and her loving son Nicky. I also believe people are brought together for very specific reasons, and often, it's only God that knows this true purpose. I do understand great loss though, and the community of people out there experiencing loss. This book will allow you to share experiences often too difficult to put words to, yet Michele still found a way to. This is courageous, and I'm sure will serve its greater purpose to help many others out there put their stories into a new context...one that can help us all."

— Michael Bell, renowned American artist
and author of DUAL LIVES.

FOREWORD

FAMILY MEMBERS OFTEN envision a loved one's journey with serious illness as a series of hash-marks that include dates of diagnosis, treatment and sometimes, a date of death as though the path was forged in steel, like a well-designed arrowhead.

What would happen if families looked at their healthcare journey as more of an adventure — one that includes a winding path complete with dangerous footing, a choice of terrain and moments of catch-your-breath beauty?

What if those same foot-soldiers knew all along that the journey never had a finish line anyway — that the concept of death as the end to a relationship is just an old-wives tale …that the truth of the matter is that there is no finish line for anyone who dies because if we love unconditionally the relationship energetically and spiritually can last forever?

Scary stuff? Maybe… because many feel that if a person's being has a firm beginning and end date, then the pain of loss will be mitigated when death occurs. What a shocker it is for these souls, that the pain of grief is only compounded by the belief that when a body dies, a relationship ends.

So how to live with death as a part of life? By breathing in the concept that the goal in any relationship is to love unconditionally. Once we open our hearts and minds to the idea that every life journey should include coursework in unconditional love, we can begin to look for teachers to guide us toward mastery of the concept.

Thankfully, we have this book, A Journey of Unconditional Love, to lean on. In it, author Michele Bell examines her son's walk with cancer and how it fused together the worst and best of the human condition. She talks frankly about her strengths and her humanity in a way that many will relate to. In these pages, we also discover the framework for living a life that uses unconditional love as the compass, the director for forward movement....something we'd all do better to rely upon.

Dianne Gray
President of Elisabeth Kubler-Ross Foundation

ONE

CANCER MOM

"I didn't become the mother I would imagine to be.
I became the mother my son needed."

THEY SAY ANGELS appear in many different ways and forms. Many people also believe that when your heart is filled with unconditional love, the persons touching your heart are angels in their own right, doing the work of angels. I believe this to be true. Unconditional love can mean something different to each of us, such as a sense of give-and-take that surrounds you or it can be a part of who you are at your core.

The power of a mother's love is beyond understanding. My soul is filled with unconditional love. In this book, I express terms of endearment without hesitation. I hope to nourish your soul with bountiful gifts of extravagant love from within. It's hard to forget someone who gave you so much to remember.

"Grief is the last act we can give to those we loved.
Where there is deep grief, there was great love."

I choose to be grateful. I embrace the pain.

"One of the most powerful forces on earth is unconditional love."

One word comes to mind that best describes this special experience of sharing and feeling true unconditional love. That word is *SELFLESSNESS*.

From the moment of a child's Divine conception, our child becomes the number one priority in our lives. This is not to say we don't stay in contact with our friends anymore or attend social events. But putting our child first provides a sense of comfort and security for all involved.

"A mother offers love that is endless, silent, and undemanding."

How does a mother who has lost a child even begin to write such a story? To recollect such horrifying events? Will words ever be able to express the emotions, the agony, or the wonder? How does one silence the millions of questions that have tormented me for years? The solidarity, the confusion, the guilt?

I will never forget the loss of my son. Not a day goes by without my soul being tugged as I live in that empty space. Space never to be refilled. Some days in public, I'll see a mother with her baby, and I'll break down. I've tried to forget. Not because I should or want to forget, but the pain taunts. The purpose of life is to love, yet my love was ripped away. What is my life without purpose? What is purpose without love?

Maybe none of the above describes you. Maybe you are more grounded and at peace. Maybe you are more forgiving. However, that certainly wasn't my story.

TWO

EMBRACE GRIEF

*"The quiet strength of a mother is to survive grief
and to continue living with half a heart."*

WITH TIME, GRIEF changes. It becomes less sharp, less jagged. Grief stays with you still, but it transmutes, becoming the fuel that inspires you.

"Grief is a dark emotion which forces us to survive."

If you feel this dawning, know that loss has the power to change you just as love has the power to uplift you. And if you are very much in the darkness of grief, know that the dawn will come—one small ray at a time.

They say the hardest thing in the world is losing a parent. I can now say, in my opinion, that's not true. The hardest thing in the world is losing a child. The loss of someone you raised, someone you taught to walk and talk, someone you showed how to love. And someone who would fall down, who disliked their broccoli, and in some cases, like my own, developed childhood cancer.

Losing a child to a terminal illness is the worst thing to happen to any parent. My reality is now my mantra, which is, 'My son transitioned.' But, before he did, he brought me so much joy. Eighteen years of being his mother taught me all the joys of loving unconditionally.

And most of all, I truly learned to live every day as if it were my last. Because, one day, it will be. Take chances and live life. Every day, tell the ones you love that you love them. Don't take any moment for granted.

Pause every day and express your thanks for your children and your parents. Revel in the time you spend with those you love most. And treat them well, because one day, when you look up from your smartphone, they may no longer be there. Be gentle with your soul. There's no time limit on grief. Unconditional love expressed outwardly can eventually help us escape from our own darkness within. Open your heart wide enough to feel joy again in honor of your loved ones, now astray. Embrace your purpose moving forward.

*"Because looking inward, and telling it like it
is, is how I've carved my own path."*

A Journey of Unconditional Love is about my son, Nicky, who lost his five-year battle with Ewing's Sarcoma, a rare form of bone cancer affecting teenagers.

My story isn't only *about* Nicky, but *for* him—to honor his brief life. I want to keep his memory alive. This book is for every family suffering from a serious illness, loss, or going through difficult times that seem insurmountable.

Whether you've endured loss or not, the pain and honesty within my tale will empower you to know you are not on your journey alone. Everyone's journey will be the only one of its kind. Unlike anyone else's. The emotions we experience are normal, even if they aren't what we expected. Holding nothing back in self-expression that heals your soul can be one way we find the path, to love, to wholeheartedly live again. Even past death, there's another way to find solace.

I can only share what I know and what I experience every day while living without my son as life forces me to embrace courage.

"Grief will never change you. Grief will reveal you.
Courage will strengthen you. I promise."

How many of us struggle with the hope of a peaceful heart after the fear of grief has consumed our soul? I say, "Faith is the only thing stronger than fear." I promise this book will empower your soul, which will carry you through your current struggles and help keep your loved ones' memory alive, just as I am doing for my Nicky.

But before I give you a glimpse into Nicky's brief life, or I share some of the statistics about childhood cancers, let me start by saying that I am not a writer. I'm just a mom who has a story to share with the world, which hopefully helps other families learn how to cope and survive even when these things seem impossible. Thank you for being willing to take a peek into Nicky's life and our family's life after he passed away.

Cancer is one of the leading causes of child death. Treatment can last years, and lengthy hospitalizations are common. The fear and anxiety for families can be endless, and families are often unprepared for the resulting emotional and financial burdens.

Through my unconditional and transcendent love connection with my son, I gained the strength to endure the unknown—day by day, minute by minute, second by second—until we were forced to let go and say our goodbyes. The journey of unconditional love I walked with Nicky showed me that, due to bountiful miracles surrounding us at every single turn, we are never alone.

"Do you ever wonder why, in a world full of miracles,
did you not get one to save your child?"

I'll share the moments of tenderness I experienced as a mother fighting each and every day to save her son's life while juggling a single parent lifestyle and raising her two children. I hope to offer comfort to you because I know firsthand what it is like to experience the daily struggle of grief. I was in a very dark place for what seemed like an eternity. My survival leads me to be a healing support for others. Providing support and comfort is what keeps me alive *each* day.

> *"No matter how badly your heart is broken,*
> *the world doesn't stop for your grief."*

THREE

LOVE BEFORE FIRST SIGHT

MY FRIEND LAURA WEST-GARRETT kind of reminds me of me. Spunk. Mothering. Sometimes alone in the world. She sent me this, confirming the many things with which we agree. Here are her words.

An exceptional young mother.

"There are countless arguments on the validity of love at first sight, but none dispel the myth quite like motherhood. Only a mother can really know what it's like to be fully, irrevocably in love with a face they have not yet seen. Only a mother can understand the unconditional love that goes beyond your faults and flaws, deeper than your mistakes. It's a perfect love that is given without needing to be earned and begins the moment she learns of your existence: love before first sight.

"As a parent, our most important but easiest job is to love our children. The love they receive shapes their character and is reflected in the love they show others. In that sense, it is clear that Michele loved Nicky deeply. His life was filled with joy, friends, and even strangers who were blessed by the light of love that radiated from him. His life touched many. His journey inspired many more. His unbreakable spirit in the face of such a crushing diagnosis is an example to still more.

"I met Michele following Nicky's death and never had the opportunity to meet him. I only know his life through the pictures, the cards and letters, and the stories of his family and friends. Those stories and pictures include many vacations, many experiences, many star-studded encounters, and an immeasurable collection of laughter and smiles. Michele and her son embraced life. They saw how fleeting and precious it was and chose not to allow the depression of that reality to spoil their time together. They used it instead to hope for the best and live tenaciously, seizing the moments they were given.

"I can't imagine the tidal wave of grief associated with losing a child, but from an outside perspective, her response was the ultimate display of love. She elected to forego her pain to promote his happiness. She placed his quality of life above all else. She selflessly gave herself to their fight.

"She was his champion. She was his cheerleader. She was his strength. Most importantly, she stood by him and loved him through it all and until the end. That is perhaps the very definition of a mother: someone who loves you before ever laying eyes on you and will continue to do so for the rest of your life. Actually, that's not entirely accurate. She will not love her son for the rest of his life. She will love him for the rest of hers…"

—LAURA WEST-GARRETT

Nick Bell with his mom, Michelle of Eastchester, in his room at New York University Medical Center. Nick is suffering from Ewing's Sarcoma and is recovering from surgery last week to remove a tumor from his right fibula.

FOUR

INSPIRED HEALER

INTUITIVE HEALING PRACTITIONER is my true calling. After Nicky's passing, I mastered my thought process in a powerful attempt to emotionally connect with humanity, the depth of human spirit. I discovered a universal life principle and Divine intelligence that I believe is our core existence.

All of this because of the power of love. Blending wisdom, life experience, devoting the rest of my natural life to embracing my purpose, releasing all resistance to grief and anguish, and helping others turn barriers into powerful life-affirming strength. Cultivating mindfulness in everyday truthful living.

My very first Healing session was a young man around Nicky's age.

His father called me one morning, frantic. "I'm in desperate need of a counselor. My son wants to commit suicide! Please, can you help him?"

I dropped everything. And within two hours, mother and son arrived for their first session. Let's call him *Mark*. I greeted the mom with a hug and shook the young man's hand.

"Welcome," I said. A gentle tone. I wanted to delay the obvious subject, keeping in mind that first-time students were coming in with a very vulnerable state of mind. I asked Mom, "Were you able to find my place easily?" She seemed nervous at first, so I offered her some water. I sat them down together to go over some paperwork and discuss anything not related to the visit.

The young man seemed despondent upon his entrance. He looked completely and utterly sad. I asked Mark if he would like to come into another room so we could begin our session. I felt nervous as well, not knowing what he would say. Maybe I wasn't prepared for this even though it had been over ten years since Nicky's transition to the other side. I badly wanted to ease his state of mind and rely on my intuition to help him through his dark time.

I leaned back in my white faux leather lounge chair, and assured him, "Whatever we discuss is confidential. It doesn't go past this door." Then I pointed directly at it. We both watched as the door opened on its own. We looked at one another.

Mark spoke first. "There have been a lot of strange things like that going on since my cousin committed suicide."

My eyes popped open, and I sat up, leaning my elbows on my knees. He had opened up the conversation.

Now I have a confession to make. I'm an empath. I mentioned my gift earlier on. I feel other people's emotions as if they're my own. So what am I to do? Completely disconnect with people? A part of my arsenal would be to divert with humor or sarcasm with varying levels of efficacy. However, during a serious session, I need to manage the vein that channels the emotions of others into me in order to understand how best to serve my students.

That said, I wouldn't change being an empath for the world because to feel is to live.

Through thick and thin, an empath is there for you— world-class nurturers. —Dr. Judith Orloff, M.D.

My gift as a mindful empath was going to make this a very interesting first healing session.

As Mark continued, he discussed the details of his cousin's

suicide, the guilt he felt, and his aspirations in life. With all that insight, I managed to magically flip the session into a comfort zone for this young man. I can honestly say that if this were a performance, I would have won an award. I was able to leverage our conversation to create a story that related to this scenario and to move his negative thoughts to a higher level and positive light.

The hair stood up on my arms throughout most of our session. This was not the boy his father had described to me three hours earlier. Mark was anxious to *live* his life and talked about his future, including a possible girlfriend, and he mourned his cousin (whom he had lost two weeks prior). His heart seemed open, and he placed trust in me—a stranger.

I believe the universe brought us together that afternoon. Mark helped me with my own grief more than he could know. I had lost my own brother to suicide a few months before this session. The heaviness I felt lifted that afternoon. Most importantly, I brought encouragement to a young man who'd been about to commit suicide.

After one hour, we completed our session. "How are you feeling, Mark?"

He got up, held his arms open wide, and gave me a hug. "Thank you so much. I feel much better."

As we walked out to greet his mom, she stood up and smiled at him, almost in tears. I said, "Your son is an amazing young man filled with such spirit."

She moved toward us and looked up into his eyes.

"You're smiling, honey! I can see a difference on your face already." Putting her hand over her mouth, she teared up.

I offered, "Let me walk you outside. It's such a beautiful day."

My heart was filled with contentment as they drove off. Who knew if I would ever see Mark again, but I was confident that he was on his way to a brighter path.

I still occasionally get calls from his mom. From our conversations, I can tell there is no sign of suicide evidenced in her son. However, in her calls, her voice still wavers to this day. "I'm so thankful. You changed our lives in just one visit. My son is doing remarkably well."

To me, this is a telltale sign from Nicky—I *am* to utilize my unconditional love as a conduit to help others.

> *Dear Time, I am so thankful for the amount of you*
> *I have already been given.* —Michele Bell

Tamara Warika shares her story:

It was midnight, a rainy, stormy night when I got the call. "Tammy? This is your mother's neighbor. Something terrible has happened," the voice said.

It was from that moment that my life was forever changed. The voice was familiar. My mother's friend and neighbor. She proceeded to tell me that my nephew, a young man of eighteen, who lived with my mother, had committed suicide. To understand the magnitude of the devastation, you must understand what a close family we were. You see, my children and my sisters' children all grew up together and were very close. All of the children were more like siblings, spending every day with each other.

For the surviving children left behind in the family, this was to be the hardest thing they could ever imagine. You can't imagine the depth of despair and pain a loss like this brings. Questions unanswered. Wondering what could have been done differently to change the past, to save a life. As if this wasn't bad enough, I was about to hear the worst thing a mother could ever hear from her son.

"Mom," he said, "I don't know what to do. All I can think about is killing myself." He was two years older than my nephew was, and they had been close since they were babies. The memories of fishing together, playing football together, playing the guitar and singing together, the last Christmas together—these memories were haunting all of us but especially him.

Now the evil that took my nephew's life was about to take my son's?

In a panic, I called his father, and we discussed the need for him to talk to someone immediately. It couldn't be just anyone. Not just a run of the mill person who asked vague cookie cutter questions. There was no time for years of therapy. I had already witnessed my nephew fall through the cracks of the mental health system. This was emergent, and we needed him healed now. We prayed.

A search found Dr. Michele Bell. I read her profile. Specializing in grief counseling. Mindfulness and healing on a spiritual level. That was exactly what we needed. When I spoke with Dr. Bell, she assured me that if she could speak to him, she believed that everything would be okay. I remember her saying, "All I need is one visit with him, and he will be okay." She got him in right away the same day.

I took him down to talk, and as I waited, while they talked, a calmness began to come over me. A panicked mess only moments before, but now I was beginning to feel faith and trust. After the appointment, my son seemed much calmer. I asked him how he felt. He said, "You know, Mom, I feel okay. Before, I felt like I was free falling, whirling out of control fast. And now I feel grounded. I feel like everything is going to be okay. "All I could think was, *Oh my God. Thank you.* I breathed a sigh of relief for the first time in a long time.

I am a mother first and foremost and am also a nurse, and I've worked in clinical settings for several years. Dr. Michele's work and type of healing have inspired me to look at healing in a different way. I have realized that there are many levels of healing that include healing of the spirit and soul as well as the physical. I have since sought out training in various healing therapies to be able to assist in healing and helping others on many levels.

This has led me to a wonderful place where I am not only able to help others but also my family and myself. When life gets rough, as it is almost always certain to be, I now feel better equipped to be able to settle my soul and be in a place of mindful peace. I can't express how much gratitude I have.

I am forever indebted to Dr. Bell for saving my son's life that day, and for inspiring me to begin this journey I'm on now. It has been two years, and my son is doing better than ever. Since that time, I have brought my mother and younger son to Dr. Michele with the same miraculous results. She has healed my family on a deep spiritual level. She has saved my family's lives and, in turn, saved mine. I am truly thankful for the gift of Dr. Michele Bell in my life.

—Tamara Warika

FIVE

THE JOURNEY

W E ARE ALL on a journey, which allows us to see our loved ones again. Until then, we must continue to honor their lives with unconditional love. My son's legacy began the moment of his conception. I carried him for nine beautiful months. I sang or hummed to him every night as he grew in my tummy. And after he was born, I thanked God for His gift every moment I looked into Nicky's big brown eyes. My little one always shared a gentle smile with me.

Our bond was transcendent from the moment he was born as the nurse placed him on my chest. When he looked into my eyes, I knew he was a unique soul. He never left my hip until the very end, on December 29, 2005. Having a son—my son—*that* I can't explain.

I vividly remember how I did everything to ensure Nicky was a healthy baby. No one was allowed to smoke in my home or around me. I'd meditate each morning and night. Remaining calm at all times and away from negative energy was challenging at times; there was a lot of conflict within the house most days. His father's thick Italian accent pierced through my veins when he expressed himself aggressively. That was usually my cue to go out for a long walk somewhere far away.

My daily dietary intake consisted of the purest of foods, lots of exercise, and most importantly, large amounts of water! From the very beginning, I wanted to make sure Nicky was grounded, mentally and as well as physically healthy.

As I waited, preparing the house for my firstborn was my goal for the remaining nine months. I wanted everything perfect. Keeping Nicky's soul at harmony, unfolding life's Divine blessings, I placed colors surrounding his crib, hues that would delight his eyes as music compositions played, and he would fall asleep.

So, although life had thrown him a curveball in his teens, Nicky *always* exuded happiness with his infectious smile. He always worried about others before himself, and he never took life for granted. Nicky was a simple soul who loved graciously and was loved very much in return. Many of his friends often mentioned they were blessed to have known him. Nicky's closest friends honored his life by getting tattoos of the inscription he wrote on a sticky note. He left it on my computer monitor one evening before he went out with his friends. It read,

> *"We are pressed on every side by troubles, but we are not crushed or broken. We are perplexed, but we won't give up and quit. We are hunted down, but God never abandons us. We get knocked down, but we get back up and keep going."*

Everyone graced by Nicky's presence admired his wisdom, hearty laugh, and his incredible smile. Through his faith, love, and respect, he projected a strong sense of how life *should* be lived. His soft voice spoke the wisdom of an old soul wrapped in a cocoon of a little, wise man.

This book is for anyone, not only for families who've suffered the loss of a child. After reading my story, my hope is that you will come to realize nothing can be taken for granted, that tomorrow is promised to no one, and the only way to live life is to recognize the worth of *everything* you have.

You don't have to have something precious taken away to wonder whether you can go on living. Consider treasuring the small, beautiful things you're given every day on a continual basis. The boundless journey you are traveling on will one day reunite you with your loved ones.

Here's a simple reminder I tend to offer up when talking with grieving parents:

"Live your life in honor of your child; celebrate death in a new light."

We must continue to act as their parent while they wait for us until we meet again…

> *Gates of memories will never close. How much we miss our loved ones, no one knows. Days will pass into years. And we'll think of those memories with silent tears.*

"Remember their soul and the way they led their lives."

Families will need to figure out lots of things on their own, and there's such a deep and satisfying reward knowing we are finding our will to face life's challenges.

> *"Entrust your heart to always rise above negative forces that attempt to enthrall your soul."*

But, there is also a lot of exhaustion and frustration over the daily struggle. In the unending vortex of single parenting, it is easy to feel like you're standing in the middle of the New York Stock Exchange trying to be heard.

The struggle… to keep going. How many days did I feel powerless?

Many! In fact, they often outnumbered my good days, and many years later, I often feel powerless. Still.

"There is a sacredness in tears. They are not a mark of weakness, but of power. They speak more eloquently than ten thousand tongues. They are the messengers of overwhelming grief, of deep contrition, and of unconditional love."

The struggle...to speak up. I couldn't find my voice. Most people would fail to believe this today, but my voice came from the perspective of firsthand experience. Losing a job, living at a friend's house on the couch, or getting turned down for government assistance. It starts by recognizing that you've been placed in a position of survival. That your opinion is valuable.

The struggle... to let go. Once a child *is* diagnosed with a terminal illness, it becomes very difficult to let go of them if, or when, they are given less time than *you* have lived on this earth.

Let them live. Give them a purpose for whatever moments may be left. Let go, Let God. Have faith. Don't smother the little bit of life they have left. My best advice—not just as a Cancer Mom, but also as a parent—is never instill fear into your child. Guidance shown with love is much more expressive. Allow yourself to become your child for a moment. Give your own fear over to a Higher Power and pray for inner guidance. If you have never prayed before, now is a good time to start. If you don't know how then ask someone or start talking aloud, but not only with *your requests*. Start by expressing gratitude and end with thankfulness, such as:

God/Higher Power,

You and I know I don't talk to you. And it might seem selfish for me to talk to you now when my needs are great—but they are great so let me start by saying I appreciate you for being here, right now. Listening to someone who should have started talking to you long ago. You gave me my son/daughter, and I have done my best, and now I need you to heal them. Or help me learn how to cope if they are not healed—and thank you for being the great healer and the great comforter. I need both now.

We, as parents, must keep our minds focused on the positive for the sake of our child's mental health.

As I think back over the last decade, I realize how blessed we were in our journey. There are times when I felt guilty for having brought Nicky into this cruel world, yet those feelings didn't last long. I have learned that—through *his* wisdom, his existence, and his path in life—I have acquired an even deeper understanding of faith for what is to prepare me for the next part of *my* journey. God called for his soul, but I will always wonder *why He did*.

I am incredibly proud to have had a son whose presence illuminated the lives of those he touched. Nicky wasn't *taken from me*—he was *given to me* in his time here.

To my son:

Thank you, Nicky, for teaching me patience, deepening my strength to continue each day without you. My loneliness, slightly alleviated, relies on my faith. Knowing that you're no longer in pain. Our souls will meet again. I feel your presence each day. You will never leave this earth while I remain. Keeping your memory alive guides others through their grieving.

I love you, Nicky.

Ma

SIX

FEARLESS CAREGIVER

MY STORY AND MY experiences as a caregiver aren't unique nor is it glamorous. My story may not seem as fancy or as well written as other stories you might have read. I'd like to tell you that this is my pleasure, but rather, this is my pain. I pour it out onto my keyboard, hoping it makes sense to you, even inspires you, but mostly—to let you know that I'm not too different from any other caregiver.

We have all loved, lost, and then loved again. We all bleed slowly and—long after the bleeding stops—we still feel the pain. Intensely. Viscerally. *When does it end?*

I admit I'm neither a nurse nor a medically trained caregiver. I may not be able to perform CPR or know one end of a thermometer from another. But what's unifying in my story is this: We loved someone, and we took care of them. And many of us lost that loved one, despite our best efforts.

I am a mom—a mom who transitioned from helping my son do his homework to helping him breathe, battle childhood cancer, and survive life. I was a very good mom. Still, all the care and love in the world wasn't enough to save his life. I *was* a mom. Now, I'm a grieving mom, still grieving eleven years after Nicky had died.

I became Nicky's caregiver, but first, I was his mom.

Nicky was born on a warm summer's day on the twentieth day of June in upstate New York. A year later, I gave birth to Bianca-Marina Ann, Nicky's sister, adding to our family. My second child, but there was something different about it. Both of my children were thriving, growing, learning, developing personal skills, and making me laugh several times a day. As I look back, I realize we had a lovely life. Nicky, a rambunctious boy—always building something, always imitating someone, always the bright spot on any dreary day.

I enjoyed being a mother. What was there for me not to enjoy? I had two healthy children. Oh sure, there was the usual common cold, scraped knee, broken wrist, mud-all-over-new-clothes, but all in all, I felt blessed. I *was* blessed. I felt that God was good to me, and I was grateful.

I remember looking at my kids and thinking, Wait a minute. They were just crawling, learning to walk, going off to grade school. Trying out for little league, and now… When did Nicky become a teenager? And Bianca following in his footsteps? Where was I when he began transitioning into manhood?

As most people do, I married and planned to have a family, but I didn't have any formal education on 'how to run a family' or 'how to do the hard stuff.' As a single mom, I had one mantra: *Nothing is impossible.* As a mother, if you know your purpose, it will make your vision clearer.

We all take it for granted that we will be caregivers to our kids. Give them all they need in life. We anticipate scraped knees, hurt feelings, measles, the flu, colds, sniffles, and maybe some bee stings. I was prepared for those early childhood inevitabilities. But I wasn't prepared for Nicky's teenage years. None of us were—least of all Nicky.

People long to grow up and move to Westchester County, New York. Suburbia. There are large homes, good schools, neighborhood parties, and sleepovers. Everyone cared about everyone there. My son, Nicky, was no exception. I was a single mom with two young children moving into a small community in the early nineties.

I didn't have any guidance on how to take care of my son when he the newly diagnosed him with Ewing's Sarcoma. Therefore, I was an unprepared caregiver. When was there time to learn what to do, what to expect, or even to ask Google? Help came in the form of friends—the Care Crew. They saw that, no matter how much I wanted to do everything for my boy, I had my daughter to take care of as well, plus myself. This was when I understood why, on airplanes, they tell parents to put the oxygen on themselves first. It did not make a difference for me in terms of ease, whether Nicky was at home or at the hospital. The round-the-clock professionals were always there to help me, yet my heart was crushed 24/7. My purpose was to go above and beyond for my children.

A few months before the escalation of Nicky's illness, I had an emergency hysterectomy, another cancer scare. Barely able to move upon returning home, we both leaned on one another for emotional support. Our unconditional love and bond transcends death, even to this day.

Back before Nicky's journey with chemotherapy, I did the basic tasks when he was a baby—feeding, cleaning, playing with him. When he was young, I did these things naturally. Once he was diagnosed with terminal cancer, I did these things to keep him alive. I had to learn some extra medical procedures such as CPR, how to operate machines, and understanding medications—it was like a crash course in nursing—but at the end, no degree, no diploma, and worst of all, no Nicky.

Wisdom, knowledge, experience, and good judgment are skills taught to a caregiver by their loved ones. Once the clock stops, we are forced to understand that acceptance is driven by unconditional love.

Our lives become punctured with emotions reeling between hope and joy as we embrace the resilience to give everything we have left inside.

There was nothing rewarding about being a caregiver to my dying teenage son because, no matter how much I did, in the end, it was the end of him. Had he survived, all the caregiving would have been rewarding. Maybe the reward is in heaven where Nicky is waiting for me. However, I didn't feel any reward.

The most difficult part of caregiving was not the sleepless nights, not the myriad of unanswered questions, nor the constant care to Nicky's physical and emotional well-being. It wasn't cleaning up vomit, late-night visits to the doctor, nor the high fevers and lying to my son, saying, "It's gonna be okay," when I knew it was not.

The most difficult part of caregiving was anytime I had a moment to myself that didn't concern Nicky—such as eating ice cream at three a.m. in the kitchen—I would feel an unbearable sense of guilt.

Difficult. To have an extra ten minutes a day would have meant taking a long hot bath surrounded by candles, lavender, and in-hand, a glass of Prosecco wine, with some of my favorite music playing on the iPod. For these ten precious minutes, someone would be with Nicky.

Did I learn anything from being a caregiver to my son, who didn't survive regardless of how much caregiving he got from anyone? Yes, I learned how to be a caregiver for my mom—who now, several years after Nicky had passed away, has latent Dementia combined with a few other ailments.

With Nicky, I cared for my son—my baby even in his teenage years. Even then, he was trying to be the adult to take care of me, even while he was dying.

Contrast that with my mom, I'm now in the role of caring for her, and her actions are like that of a child though she's an adult.

The relationship between my mom and me has always been an endless struggle. So many families can end up with values that are very different. Values become what you believe in your core. We're very different. At the very core, she's been a selfish person her entire life. And although I am her daughter, I'm the complete opposite. I became her caregiver, and thus, out of obligation and my deep belief in doing what is proper by your loved ones, I take care of her as I did Nicky.

In 2013, I left my life, memories, and career to move back into the family home I'd run away from thirty years before. My loving life partner, whom I met three months after Nicky transitioned in 2005, joined me in this loyal quest of caregiving for my mom.

In the beginning, it was a nightmare. My mother would purposely stir up excitement—within the house, among the neighbors, and inside the church—causing stress among us all, including my partner.

Her driving skills were never the greatest. She'd fly through stop signs and red lights, well before she was even diagnosed with Dementia. This didn't give us a clue about the coming problem. She would always think it was funny and laugh, "Your old lady is a violator, Michele. Get over it." Shaking my head, I would agree.

Years into caregiving for my mom, she remained a physically active eighty-two-year-old, even attending church seven days a week.

Shortly after we moved, there was a rumor circulating—possibly within our local church community—that I had moved home to steal her money, her house, and put her in a nursing home. The verbal harassment I received each day was toxic.

However, the fact was, a close neighbor and friend had informed me via telephone that something wasn't quite right with my mom. So I drove up from Westchester to begin the chore of seeing for myself what might be wrong. By taking her to various specialists, we found out she was in the mid stages of Dementia.

It's been five years now since we moved in, and my partner and I are with her 24/7 in her family home per her wishes.

I love Mom dearly. However, my most difficult pillar was *acceptance.* We have absolutely nothing in common, yet I try my hardest to gain her approval each day by offering to do the things she would normally do.

Her weekly manicures, pedicures, and hair appointments are fun for her and good for her socializing skills. Movies were her favorite hobby. I get a kick out of how she'd hop into another movie at the theater if she didn't like one she'd paid to see. Deep down, I have always wished she was able to calmly enjoy our shared moments together.

I admit I struggled on so many levels with her personality. So grateful that now my emotions like that are behind me. Taking care of someone who lacks genuine heart can be rough on the psyche, especially as it escalates daily.

Watching her is hard on two levels—dementia took mom further away from me. And if someone isn't pleasant, it can be a good thing—unless that unpleasantness to you remains. And with Mom, it seemed it did. Maybe her unhappiness is all she had for me.

With the church and neighbors, Barbara isn't the same at all—for them, she could be a different person. And that's the second part I had to deal with.

Imagine having one last chance to try to get someone to treat you with kindness, to love you, to see you just a little better, only to find this person has gone to a place you cannot reach.

My mom gave up my older brother for adoption when she was twenty-five years old. I learned of this when I was thirty, and I found him through the adoption registry. We remained closely connected until late this past summer when he committed suicide at the age of fifty-seven. He was a prominent attorney in Denver, Colorado, with a huge heart for animals.

Although my brother, Michael Jude, met our mom years into his adulthood, he had a history of depression and anxiety. He confessed his history to me in a text. He felt disconnected and abandoned. I took on the "mom" role to him for many years out of guilt. I was never fond of the choice my mother had made, but I didn't live her life, and only she can absolve herself for that.

I could sense he was in so much pain as I would read his texts and during our late-night chats. Over the months leading up to his dreadful suicide, I knew his soul was in desperate pain. He offered to help me care for my mom by asking us all to move to Denver to commune as a family.

Obviously, that never happened. My heart was torn.

∞

MOM IS ALWAYS in constant movement—unlocking the door, running to the neighbor's next door to smoke, or taking off if I'm doing laundry—I now do my best to keep her in check. I don't want to take away any daily activities she's used to doing. At this point, my decision is to keep her home.

No matter how good I was at my job of being "Caregiver Mom" or "Caregiver Daughter," in the end, I will lose both my patients: my son first, and now my mother may not be here much longer.

The balance I must work at to help her maintain *her* equilibrium is similar to going on a diet. It is easy to diet when you're rewarded weekly with weight loss and increased self-esteem. When all that is over, you know your sleepless nights of caregiving are worth it. You have a pain-free healthy child at home. A happy mother you've cared for. In my case, I don't have my son, and soon, I won't have my mom, either.

My mother and my son. My son. My mother. Connected by one person—me. Two totally different views of two different lives. You would think Nicky's wouldn't be the same as my mother's life. Yet, despite all of his struggles, there is much irony to his story, as well.

SEVEN

THE BUMP

NICKY, MY 13-YEAR-OLD eighth-grader was playing right-guard representing our county village and community. I sat in the stands cheering him on. His determination was a sight to see! I was so proud!

It was a Friday evening late in March 2001, and I, a proud parent, sat among others watching the game unfold as players moved fluidly up and down the court. I loved watching Nicky play. He wasn't the biggest or tallest kid on the court, but he was a real spitfire. With long skinny legs, he was very agile, not to mention extremely focused.

He had always been very athletic, enjoying hockey, skateboarding, baseball, and skiing. He typically embraced any challenge. But, unfortunately, no child is up for the challenge of fighting for his or her own life. However, Nicky was a fighter until the very end.

I've come to realize that, unlike other mothers watching their child fight to win a game, Nicky's fight was soon to be on a much larger scale. He wouldn't be fighting another community team on a court or field—his foe would be fighting cancer, fighting for his life. I've since wondered daily, "How does a teenager do that?"

Trying to save his life over the next five years would be the ultimate challenge for *any* parent. I cheered him as he played basketball, but he was the one playing this new game. Standing on the sidelines as his cheerleader soon would become a full-time role, much more than just rooting to win the game. This was a basketball game unlike *any* other. Nicky verses Team Cancer.

Although I was single and working non-stop to support two kids, I went to as many of Nicky's games as I could. Since he started bouncing the ball and learning the technique, he had loved the sport like any other child. He went to the court with his friends every chance he got, and he had played on teams since elementary school. In the summer, Nicky would go to basketball camps. He loved sports immensely, particularly basketball.

About halfway through the game, Nicky was fiercely running with the ball down the court. I watched him dribble past an opposing player, lunging to get possession when the other boy accidentally kicked Nicky in the leg so hard my son collapsed. At that moment, I frantically ran down the bleachers and into the middle of the court.

Nicky was lying flat on his back, holding his leg. The referee hadn't blown the whistle and players swirled around us. I looked up and around me with a cold, blank stare. *Is anyone going to help me with my son? Are they going to stop the game?*

I shook my head while my son was holding his leg to his chest in pain. Amid the dribbling and shouting, I tried to help him sit up. Nicky's facial expression, along with low tones of grunting, indicated how much pain he was in—the most pain I had ever witnessed him experience. There was *no* question in my mind—he *had* to come out of the game.

"Nicky, c'mon, let's go home," I declared.

My hands roamed his limbs, checking for any broken bones. I was frustrated that no one else had reacted after he'd fallen so hard. I watched the boy who had kicked him. *Did he do it on purpose?*

As we sprawled in the middle of the court, I insisted we either go to the hospital or step out of the game. Like all teens, I got the standard, adamant, "No, Ma. I just want to finish the game."

I argued, "We need to go to the hospital." Even *I* could see the amount of pain he was in.

"Ma, please. I'm okay! Please, let me play the rest of the game," he argued. His tenacity and sense of loyalty were so strong, way above that of anyone else in his age group.

Looking back, I see the irony now.

I nodded, hugged him, and just said, "Okay, sweetheart, all is good. You'll be fine." I didn't want to make him feel any more insecure for fumbling in the game.

My son was a strong-willed and determined person. He finally got to his feet and forced himself to continue, limping his way up and down the court. It was difficult to watch.

I suspected he felt loyal to his teammates and wanted to prove to them that he'd never let them down. His loyalty and dedication eased my concerns, and soon, this incident was of little concern. I told myself it was a minor injury that we'd both soon forget.

∞

WHEN WE RETURNED home later that evening, Nicky hobbled in, still limping and holding his leg. Needless to say, I was concerned. This wasn't like him. Nicky had been bumped and had fallen before. It is all part of the game. Yet, this time, something was different. Normally, no matter how many times he was jabbed with an elbow, tripped, fouled, fallen, he would rebound and, within seconds, all would be forgotten. That wasn't the case this time.

That night, I watched my son experience tremendous pain, and no mother likes to see that. "Nicky," I reasoned with him, "you have to get that looked at by a doctor. Let's go to the hospital."

"No, Ma, it's okay." That was all I could get from him. He was tired and just wanted to sleep.

I didn't press it because, overall, he seemed to be all right. Instead, I grabbed a bandage and wrapped it around his leg. It was all he would let me do. He wore the bandage to school for the remainder of the week.

I thought *it* could *just be a muscle pull*. A few days later, a bruise appeared lower down his right leg on the outside. But Nicky assured us, "I'm not in pain."

My intuition led me to take him to the emergency room anyway, to have an x-ray verify that there was no bone damage as I suspected. But his bone was intact, and there was no inflammation. The medical team suggested we follow up with his pediatrician a few weeks later.

And so we did. Dr. Sutton examined Nicky and found no signs of an injury.

So, naturally, I thought he had recovered. Looking back, I wonder if I should have been stronger. To this day, that bump haunts my dreams. *Would things have been differen*t?

Nicky finished the basketball season, and before we knew it, spring had arrived, and life had moved forward.

∞

WITHOUT KNOWING THE horrid news to come, we continued with our lives as planned. In May 2001, we went on vacation over Mother's Day weekend. Nicky seemed his usual self—enjoying life, having a blast on his skateboard, and running around on the sand with his dog, Lily. I invited my mother to come down for the weekend, and we all drove to the Hamptons.

That weekend was a memory I will always treasure. Surrounded by my son's boundless love and energy, I was so happy we were together. Nicky's sister had decided to spend the holiday upstate with her dad that weekend, so Mom, Nicky, and I were together for a time, sharing memories.

Nicky was skateboarding fluidly across the driveway of our private, dog-friendly bed and breakfast, steps away from the ocean. Watching from afar, his playing with Lily on the beach always brought happiness to my heart. No matter what he was doing, happiness exuded from him, and his smile was contagious.

I missed my daughter very much that weekend, and I made up for it a few weeks later by taking both kids to Cape Cod.

In June, after his eighth-grade graduation, Nicky traveled back and forth to visit his father and grandmother in upstate New York for the summer. I was so proud of my son, who was now entering a new period of his life. These were the times during which teenagers plan their future. However, Nicky was about to fight for his.

Nicky's father and I had been divorced for several years with visitation arrangements always flexible and honored. So I'd arranged for the kids to go upstate, based on what their school and summer activity schedule would allow. For some reason, it seemed Nicky would always call me and want to come home. However, I always encouraged him to spend time with his father. I didn't want to be seen as being uncooperative since I always allowed them to see their father any time to avoid added stress.

Although Nicky's roots began in upstate New York, he was always more drawn to his small community in Westchester. The outpouring of friends and genuine loyalty proved this. Even later, Nicky was regarded as a backbone for strength and loyalty, not the "kid with cancer." He wanted *no* part of any pity party.

By the time Nicky left for his trips upstate that summer, the bruise on his leg had disappeared entirely. I then thought it was nothing more than a painful but fleeting childhood injury.

∞

JULY AND AUGUST passed uneventfully until his father called about a week before Nicky had to return back downstate to begin his high school journey.

On our call, his father explained in a heavy Italian accent, "Nicky's got a bump on his leg." Rocco, Nicky's cousin, and Nick were playing video games, and Rocco was the one who noticed it.

Hearing this, my main question came a bit fast and strong. "Did you take him to see a doctor?"

Nicky's dad talked over me, loud and firm. "I'm sending him back down so you can take him to the doctor."

I calmly requested he drive Nicky back downstate immediately. I felt he should've taken Nicky for observation that day. This way, the results could be sent to his downstate doctor to begin the process. His voice pierced my ear as he wouldn't stop yelling in the phone.

I yelled back, "How can you be taking this so lightly? I want Nicky home by tomorrow!"

He said, "I have no car. And I'm working."

My fiery rebuttal remained unspoken. Seething as I wanted to release my wrath on him, but I didn't. He probably had more to say, too, but he held back.

I wasn't sure if the bump he was referring to was in the same area where Nicky was hit during the basketball game. And I wouldn't know for sure until he'd returned home from his father's place.

My gut told me to drop everything and drive up to get my son home right away. I felt we needed to get him to a doctor. I was sure there hadn't been a bump on his leg when he graduated eighth grade. Neither had I noticed a bump over Mother's Day nor before he'd left in June after his graduation.

Nicky arrived home a few days later, and to my surprise, I saw the bump was exactly in the same place he was hit that evening at school. It was the size of a grapefruit on the outside of his right leg.

I called Dr. Sutton immediately, and he saw Nicky the next day.

The answers to this mysterious bump were certainly not what I would have expected to hear.

I was devastated.

I sat there asking myself several questions. Could this be related to the kick he received during that basketball game? But his leg was only swelling up now, almost five months later. How could one accidental kick do this to my son? And why was the bump so large?

My thoughts grew and grew.

Even though his dad had contacted me, why did he now seem to be so alarmed? How long had he known it was like this?

I later found out that Nicky had told his father about the pains, but my son called them "growing pains." I suspect that maybe Nicky knew something serious was going on, but he was the type of person who kept his troubles to himself, not wanting to burden anyone. At the time, he wore his shorts pretty far below the knee, which was the style for kids so his dad may not have noticed anything until it was impossible *not* to notice.

Again, I looked at the photos of that Mother's Day on our mini-vacation in the Hamptons with my mother, Nicky, and our dog, Lily. I didn't notice *any* bump in any photos. There he was, running with our Lily and skateboarding, doing flips in the air. Nothing prompted an injury, and nothing hinted that he was in pain.

Dr. Sutton was our pediatrician in New Rochelle. "I can't even look at that," the doctor said. "You need to take him to see an orthopedic bone specialist immediately. I'll recommend one for you. He's located in Scarsdale. You'll be in good hands. He'll take good care of your son, but there's nothing I can really do at this moment. Nicky will need further evaluation."

Upon leaving the office, I knew there was something devastatingly wrong. I was shaking inside with fear. My instincts led me to believe this was something *way* beyond my control, and Nicky knew something wasn't right.

"Ma, is everything okay?"

Firmly grasping my steering wheel, I wanted to scream.

"Yes, Nicky. Everything is fine." The same infamous words I had said to my children all their lives.

I went home, got on the computer, and started doing some research. The recommended specialist was rated the top bone guy in the area and had remarkable credentials. He was the Chief of Musculoskeletal Oncology of Orthopedic Surgery at various hospitals throughout Long Island and New York City.

I felt at ease so far, until our visit the following day.

Nicky had been out for his first week already. A freshman and he hadn't even been able to put books in his locker. I had made Nicky lunch just before our appointment as we sat at the dining room table together. All of a sudden, he looked up at me while slurping his noodles.

"Ma, will I be able to go back to school like the other kids?" With a big smile, I looked at him, nodding my head.

"Don't worry about it," I reassured him. "There is no reason for you not to go to school, but we need to follow up on this bump, Nicky. Let's get through this appointment together, and then we'll get through whatever this obstacle may be and move on with our lives."

I got up from the table, took his bowl, and suggested he play his Xbox games to take his mind off worrying. I always managed to sidetrack any negative thoughts with positive reinforcement.

Upon entering the waiting area, I noticed all the "Best Doctor" awards plastered all over the wall.

"Look, Nicky, he seems to be on his game with all these!" I noted. "So there's no need to worry."

Slow breaths, I kept saying to myself as we waited inside the room. Praying within, I asked for a white light to surround our anxiety because my strength was depleting.

There was a gentle knock on the door accompanied by a soft voice with an accent. "Hello, my name is Dr. Kenan. And this must be Nick."

Nicky got up and shook his hand before sitting back down. He asked Nicky to jump up onto the table so he could examine his right fibula. I stared at his facial expression, then at Nicky's large bump, attempting to analyze what Dr. Kenan might say next.

Would it be good news or bad news?

He seemed slightly encouraged. At least he wasn't frowning as he felt the entire area of Nicky's leg. Dr. Kenan specifically asked, "Had there been an accident?" I *immediately* stood up. "Perhaps, in the area of where I'm examining."

In a stern voice, I proclaimed, "Yes! There was!" I then explained Nicky had played in a school game this past March and got kicked in the leg. At that moment, he explained that Nicky would need to have surgery to determine whether or not the bump was benign. Then the thoughts wouldn't stop coming.

What the hell does benign mean? What could this mean for us down the road? What if it isn't benign?

Dr. Kenan was kind and gentle with his words, but he worked swiftly to schedule a procedure at Beth Israel Hospital in New York City to find out what was going on. I saw it as a standard procedure, but my inner spirit signaled me to prepare for the worst.

Nicky asked many questions, but nonetheless, I always tried to give vague answers and not go into details. My son was still a young child, and I tried to protect him. I didn't want him to become anxious or scared. I answered his questions in a light, gentle, positive way, reinforcing that everything would be okay. However, *my* insides were a bundle of nerves ready to explode. I needed to compose myself.

"Nicky, you're going to have a small operation," is how I explained things. "It's no big deal. They're going to go into your leg to find out what's wrong so they can make you better."

What do you say to a frightened teenager when your insides are ripping part? I was *beyond* devastated. In fact, I truly felt *helpless*. All I could imagine was whatever was taking over my son's body could be injected into me, instead. *Please, just let it be me—and not him!*

My mother drove down from Upstate New York the night before and came with us for the biopsy. It was scheduled for a Friday morning at seven a.m. at Beth Israel. I had a driver come pick us up to alleviate the stress, allowing us moments of undivided attention. The drive to the hospital wasn't entirely serious as my mother *always* lights up a room with her silly sense of humor. But still, we didn't talk much. I could sense Nicky was alarmed. I could tell because of the way he reached for my hand, both wishing his sister and father were with us.

After the long process of checking in, Nicky waited, ready for the biopsy.

Finally, one of the nurses came out into the waiting area. She yelled, "Nick Bell!" We all stood up.

I asked if I could go with him, but she explained, "We need to prep him for outpatient surgery."

How do you allow such a young boy to be without his mother for comfort? I wondered.

I gave him a big hug and a kiss on the forehead.

Barbara gave him her sign of the cross on his forehead with a grandmotherly kiss as a chaser.

I told him, "We'll see you in a while. You're going to be fine, babe," as I squeezed his hand.

My mother and I waited and waited, and then we waited some more. I stared at the big black and white clock in the waiting area. The numbers and the spaces. Pacing, finally walking outside for air. As I walked out and stared at the sky above, tears poured from my eyes.

I asked whoever was in charge to allow Divine intervention to positively come forth for my son. Hours had passed. And I started to feel nervous because I didn't expect them to be so long. I kept imagining what might be going on. That's when the anxiety really started to kick in.

After almost three hours, Dr. Kenan came out. In a very professional and compassionate way, he asked us to sit so we could discuss his findings. From the way he looked at me, I *immediately* knew something was wrong.

"Through the biopsy," he said, "I've found that your son has a rare bone cancer. It's called Ewing's Sarcoma."

I couldn't say a word. I just stared. I watched his mouth keep moving, but I didn't hear a word of what he said. It was as if the words had stood still, and I was frozen in time. The only word screaming through my mind was *CANCER!*

Then, I heard my mother next to me anguished, her voice saying, "What are we going to do? How are we going to take care of this?"

This was the beginning of the worst nightmare of our lives.

EIGHT

PRAYING FOR A BOY

A S WE DROVE home from just hearing the most devastating news of our lives, I reconnected with my greatest passion in life, which was to have children and to be a mom.

My mind was still back there in the waiting area of the hospital, many people surrounding us. Through the hubbub, my mind felt blank, suddenly racing to places I couldn't stop it from going. I thought to my precious son, and then to how I didn't have a pleasant childhood. I never had a chance to know my dad well at all. This is why I ensured my children were fully exposed to their father, no matter what the circumstances. I would never disengage their relationship. I would only encourage it.

Throughout most of my life, I believed I had no siblings. It wasn't until years later that I found out I had *three* siblings. Round and round unconnected thoughts filled my brain.

Would Nicky never get to ruminate like I was doing right now? Even that came to me, as I tried to avoid the word the doctor had just laid on my heart: *Cancer.*

And still, my mind whirled around my past rather than face living in the now.

Because I didn't grow up with siblings, I grew up a very lonely child. I lived with a controlling mother who I despised for many years. From a young age, I longed to be a mother to create the family I never had for myself. After I became pregnant, every night during those months, I prayed for a boy. Having only a loose bond with my father, I longed for a male presence in my life.

As I said before, I made sure to take care of myself during my pregnancy. I never smoked, nor let anyone smoke around me. I never drank, I ate very healthily, and I exercised. I went to all my childbearing classes and prepared carefully for my child's birth. I guess I was a bit obsessive. Subconsciously, I assumed that if I took the utmost care of my unborn child, our lives would blossom. However, the future was not what I had expected.

∞

NICKY WAS DELIVERED by Dr. Pardinani in Bellevue Hospital in 1987. My excruciating labor lasted thirty hours. But every minute was worth the pain. I vividly remember taking endless walks up and down the hospital's hallways as I prepared for this very painful, yet blessed, experience. By my bed was a cassette recorder playing soothing meditation music.

With my rosary beads laid out, holy water, and a statue of the Virgin Mary on the bed table, I came prepared. I'd always been a spiritual person because of how I was raised. Catholic schools and weekly Sunday mass were instilled in me at a young age. I remember admiring my grandmother, as she gracefully dressed for church each week. She was a genuine, kind soul. I admired her devotion each day as she engaged in the true spirit of faith. I would listen to her do her rosary every single day while cleaning as I watched television. She kept to herself, often timid, yet sincerely felt. These are the moments I remember that helped me get through the obstacles.

However, while I am fortunate for the structured religious practice, I'm now less involved in formal religion and instead, more involved in my own spiritual beliefs. I'm someone who's discovered that what lights me up is helping others see what lights *them* up. By sharing my story, I live for the sole purpose of celebrating the Divine light in each of us.

Dr. Umku had given me an epidural that night, but still, I was now into ten long hours of labor. Being petrified of needles, I'll never forget the shot straight to my spine. I can still remember hugging my mother and saying, "Jesus, help me. Please, Jesus, help me."

To lighten the mood, Dr. Umku had assured me with a murmured, "Jesus is coming, Michele."

Just hearing this gave me a sense of relief. For the final stages of birth, it helped to calm me down as I prepared.

With the painkiller, a sense of calm came over me. I directed my attention to the television. *The Price is Right* was on. At the time, I had a little crush on Bob Barker. I once saw his show in person. He had struck me as a little guy on a big stage with a tan to die for.

As I breathed in all the ways I was supposed to and watched Bobby work his magic, I couldn't help but think about the magic of giving birth. Watching Nicky's dad pacing outside in the hallway talking to himself allowed me to find the peace to compose my inner thoughts. I was planning Nick's future, the things we would do together, and so much more.

I was wheeled into a large, cold room where everyone wore a mask. I was petrified.

"Push, push, push," the doctor chanted. Absolutely gentle, very calm and soothing—so gentle I didn't even know the second that Nicky was born. And then, there he was. My son, Nicky.

He didn't make a sound. No screaming or crying like on television. Instead, my boy was extremely quiet and calm. The nurse put him on my chest. I looked at him, and he looked at me. It was an *incredible* moment.

And now, *now*, I would have to see that little peanut face again and explain all of this. Now, I'd have to explain the situation to my beautiful boy.

The night he was born, Nicky seemed like a little peanut, with his jet-black hair and big brown eyes. At 7 pounds, 4 ounces, I listened intensely to every baby sound he made. He was quiet, but loud enough for the two of us. It was like music to my ears. That was how Nicky had been his whole life: A happy kid, always smiling and laughing. *Everything* made him happy.

∞

AFTER HE WAS born, I thanked God for answering my prayers and bringing this boy into my life. When we left the hospital, I dressed him in a nautical outfit and hat, and my mother instantly nicknamed him "Skipper," a name that stuck with him throughout his life.

The doctor called me a lucky mother because I had such a quiet, relaxed baby.

Throughout the first months, I learned how to become a mother. My first days with Nicky felt exciting. I loved spending time alone with him—holding and touching him. Nicky was *so* responsive to my voice and touch.

I had never felt as close to anyone as the times I held Nicky in my arms. He would hold my fingers tightly and stare at me while I talked and sang to him. I rocked him to sleep and hummed, "You and Me Against the World" by Helen Reddy. He would try to sing back to me in baby talk. His stare felt so intense—as if I had been reunited with him in some way.

∞

FOR THE FIRST three months, he slept in my grandmother's family cradle. Nicky *never* woke up crying. In fact, he rarely cried, except when he was hungry, wet, or tired. In the mornings, he always woke up babbling to himself, waiting for me to come for him. I remember I would lie in bed listening to his voice while he played quietly in his crib. During these moments, I felt so thankful for this precious blessing. I remember when he first stood up in his crib, holding on tight, wobbling, trying to keep his balance.

And now there was *this*. How would we keep *our* balance through all of *this*?

All through the ordeal, thoughts would come to me, comforting me, how Nicky's life had filled our memories with light and innocent moments. I'm not sure how old he was, under one, I think, but one time, after pooping in his diaper, he finger-painted the entire white-canopied crib! Such breathtaking moments filled the mosaic of his life to be bumped up against moments of procedures to come. The golden and light, wedged alongside the hardest of stone to bang our heads against, fighting this.

Thinking back to his days of chemotherapy, his good friend, Joelle, reminded me of her favorite Nicky memory: Nicky tied a string to a crumpled $5 bill, and inside the crevices was dog poop. As I think back, I actually remember the day he came home to tell me the story. I had to cross my legs, I was laughing so hard.

> *"Ma, I'm going to the video shop's parking lot to skateboard. Do you have any sewing thread and five dollars?"*

> *"I think so, Nicky. Let me go downstairs and check."*

> *As I walked upstairs, he was laughing as he folded up a small brown bag. I never questioned his silliness. A few hours later, he came home to show me the video on his flip phone explaining what he did.*

> *"Ma, I added that string you gave me to the five-dollar bill and put Lily's poop on the end of it.*

> *Some guy followed it all the way down the aisle in the video shop and picked it up and put it in his pocket."*

> *I have to admit when he told me, I was crying and snorting with laughter. Anything Nicky did was*

harmless, and if it brought laughter into his life, I was on the same side no matter what.

So if you were reading this story, and you answered your doorbell, but no one was there except for a burning brown bag,

I confess that could have been a Nicky prank.

At that moment, Joelle reminded me how our humorous bond was always in sync. This was definitely my son. Joelle continued to tell me that guy finally caught the $5 bill and shoved it in his pocket.

Nicky was the master jokester in the community

When Nicky couldn't have been more than three, he always wanted to be on the move, always doing something active. He would follow me from room to room while I got ready for work each day. He loved playing hide-and-seek in empty boxes. Curious about life, he also enjoyed watching me cook. He was playful, and he loved to be chased around the playground or yard. He'd laugh hysterically.

Nicky was a fussy eater. He loved peanut butter, and he would smear it all over his hands and face. He also loved to be self-sufficient, and he always wanted to learn. While he brushed his teeth, got dressed, or was eating, he was always saying, "I can do it, Mommy!" I loved his curiosity and sense of new adventure.

∞

NICKY'S SISTER WAS born eleven months after him. Bianca was really good at antagonizing Nicky to get what she wanted. I was always overly protective of Nicky's heart. While I worked from home I observed closely the dynamics of sibling playtime. When she teased Nicky while he quietly played with his toys by taking them away and saying, "Mine, these are mine," I became annoyed, especially when her father would not reprimand her in Nicky's defense.

As Nicky got older, he learned to handle Bianca's antics. He struggled during his last years, months, and days leading up without his sister fully present. It broke my heart to see him sulking when she decided to come visit on December 20. As we were getting ready for his holiday party, Bianca graced us with her presence. It was a joyous moment for all, including Nicky. His happy tears rolled off his face like a waterfall.

There was some tension when the children were four and five years old, and I needed a distraction. I arranged to host an exchange student from Bogota, Columbia. Her name was Ximena, and she was sixteen years old, beautiful, young, and innocent, now experiencing "America" in our home. Her shiny brown hair was all one length, and she was very pretty, until…

One night, as we were all nestled in our beds, the house was quiet, and we were all sleeping peacefully, Nicky's sister, Bianca, who was about four years old at the time, took my haircutting scissors and decided to become a hairdresser.

It was early in the morning, and her father had just got home from work. On that dreadful early morning, my daughter decided to cut Ximena's hair while she was sleeping. Then she cut Nicky's, too. When Ximena woke up, she noticed—and screamed. That evening, when I bathed Nicky, I lifted up his thick hair and saw three bald spots.

I asked, "What happened to your hair?"

He told me, "Ganca did it."

"Why?" I asked.

He said, "To be like Jean-Claude Van Dam. She said she'd make me look like him."

I decided to go ahead and shave his entire head. That way, when his hair grew back, it would all be the same length.

I will never forget my mother's comment when she saw him for the first time after the shave. Her remark was eerily prophetic, as she exclaimed, "What happened? He looks like a cancer patient."

A few months later, the kids were playing in the backyard. I was working while their dad was taking a shower. I was later informed that Nicky told his sister, who was standing on our picnic table, "You can fly like Tinkerbell. I want to see you fly."

Bianca listened—and she flew off the table onto the ground and broke her leg. I often worry, wondering if that might have been Nicky's way of innocently getting back at his sister after she cut his hair to the scalp, making us shave his head bald. It was devastating to shave off all his beautiful thick hair.

The three months of watching his hair grow in when he was five years old were painless when compared to the experience of watching his hair fall out all by itself in his teenage years due to his chemo treatments.

They were so young here, you can see the love.

NINE

WE'VE GOT THIS TOGETHER

THE BONE DOCTOR, Dr. Kenan told me, "Nicky will need to be admitted to NYU the following Monday morning. Dr. Rausen is one of the leading Ewing's Sarcoma oncology experts in the world."

As he told me this, I felt dazed, still *shocked* by the news, and I was also angry. Everything shut down, and again, I simply stared at his moving lips, unable to concentrate on his words.

How dare you tell me my son has cancer! I wanted to scream. It's just a kick in the leg while playing basketball! How does it go from a kick to cancer?

I'm not sure what made me start focusing again. I let these words sink in, and nodded, *yes*. Perhaps it was a mother's instinct or knowing once all this talking was finished, I'd be allowed to see my son. I excused myself.

∞

I STEPPED OUTSIDE and tried to collect my thoughts. How would I tell my Nicky what was going on?

Telling him was *my* job. Now, the only thing spinning in my mind was: *What would I say and how would I say it?*

With Nicky in the recovery room and my mother behind me in the waiting space, I needed to figure it out fast so my son didn't feel my fear and anxiety. I couldn't let him see the pain I was in. For the next fifteen minutes, I stood outside Beth Israel Hospital. I cleared my eyes and steadied my voice.

"I don't know how I am going to do this," I said. I closed my eyes and internally spoke to my higher power.

Please guide me through your spirit and give me strength. Please wrap your loving arms around us during these tender moments that are upon us.

As I opened my eyes, I felt a little lighter. I stared at people walking on the NYC streets and wondered, by the looks on some of their faces, if they seemed unhappy with their lives. I wanted to be the first to remind them of how precious life is.

How many faces am I looking upon who actually realize how valuable all life's moments are? I wondered, gazing. I heard only dead silence.

Will my children overcome the fight ahead of us as a family? I questioned. I was crushed.

During these moments, I realized I had no more time to waste. My son was waiting for me upstairs, and I had to transform into "Super Cancer Mom"—because the future was a big unknown. My only choice was to turn this devastation into a positive. I got myself together, took a huge breath, and went back inside.

As soon as I saw my mother, she let me know, "Nicky's calling for you."

All I could feel was pressure. When I tried to catch my breath, my heart was pumping so hard I could feel it beat through my chest. Walking toward his room, I felt my body filling with tears, or should I say sweat?

And so began Act One of my new role.

As soon as I entered the recovery room, all I heard was Nicky yelling for me, "Mommy! Mommy, I'm over here! Follow my voice."

I called, "I'm coming, Nicky! Mommy is coming."

Although tears welled in my eyes, I put on a happy face for him. I was *dying* inside. I walked with my arms up in the air like a cheerleader. Smiling from ear to ear, I wrapped my arms around him tight.

"Hey, Nicky, look at you—you look so handsome!"

He was very alert and excited to see me. I made sure to speak first in case my mother intervened with a strange question or comment.

"You're going to be fine," I encouraged.

"What'd they do?" Nicky asked.

I replied, "The biopsy, and you're going to have another operation on Monday because they're going to try to get rid of the bump."

His response was, "Mommy, did they get it all out?"

"The doctor's going to take care of everything," I said, reassuring him. I then took a deep breath and added, "We also have to use special medicine to make your bump shrink."

Quickly flipping the conversation to avoid any questions, I repeated how handsome he looked and that we would be going home soon. I felt the adrenaline surging through my body, holding the fear I knew would soon touch my son.

I didn't say the word "cancer." I kept the conversation focused on getting the bump removed. I kept him sheltered from the truth, but what other option was there?

"Are we ready to go home?" he asked.

"Yeah, Nicky."

"Oh good, I want to play basketball."

"Okay, honey, whatever you want."

It being an out-patient surgery, we got him dressed. "We'll talk more about everything that's going on when we get home," I assured.

As we drove back up the FDR into Westchester, all I could do was stare out the window, balancing my emotions, trying desperately not to cry. Thankfully, my friend Gino arranged for one of his drivers to take us to NYC for the procedure. There was no way I could drive myself.

Nicky and I sat in the backseat, both staring out the window.

Nicky was so in-tune with himself, he possessed the kind of self-awareness that most children his age don't.

What is he thinking? I pondered. He sat still for most of the ride. I, on the other hand, wanted to scream.

I could feel his emotions and sense his fear.

Is this some sort of punishment? I wondered. *What did we do so badly that we are faced with a "Go To Jail" card?* The thoughts racing through my head were endless as I clenched my son's hand throughout the drive.

While sitting in bumper-to-bumper traffic, my mind created a plan of action while my heart race.

How is this going to be possible? I asked myself. How do I explain to a teenager what cancer is or means when I honestly do not even know myself? I'd never been exposed to this illness in my lifetime, so I was not familiar with it.

As my body filled with anger, pondering these thoughts, I was ready to rip my fake nails off with my teeth.

Where is this kid who kicked my son on the basketball court? I demanded internally. I wanted to find out who he was. I wanted to ask him, "Why? What were you thinking?"

In an instant, I realized how negative I was being, and so I asked my higher power to focus on a positive formula for the remainder of the day.

Finally, as we approached Westchester, I felt a warmth surround my soul. Internally psyching myself up to not only think positively, but I also needed to be aggressively motivated by this illness. I *refused* to allow cancer to consume our lives, especially my family, friends, and most of all, Nicky.

∞

AS WE APPROACHED the driveway, the mood was quiet when we arrived. Nicky's sister was still in school. My mother went downstairs to do the laundry. As I prepared lunch for us, I remember that being alone in the kitchen was the only moment I had to myself. Nicky was watching television. This was *my* moment to finally burst into tears. Standing above the sandwich, folding Nicky's favorite deli meats, tears poured out, literally dripping off my face as I leaned over the counter. I could feel the heat building up in my face. My nostrils were exploding.

Raw emotions spilled out, spewed in utter sadness until there was no more anger. I was a now officially a Cancer Mom.

Later that afternoon, my mother drove back upstate. After school, Nicky's sister went to her friend Joelle's—it was a typical day for everyone else, but not for us. I took the day off from work, and Nicky was off from school. He lay sprawled on the couch, eating his lunch, waiting for me to soothe his inner fear.

I sat on the couch next to him.

"Nicky," I chose my words carefully while holding his little hand.

I spoke in a soft, gentle tone. "I don't want you to be upset or scared. I want you to know that we're going to take care of this. And everything's going to be okay. But the doctor found that you have cancer. We're going to get this out of the way. I don't want you to worry."

He was in his typical position on the couch, rolled in a ball as usual, but now I saw that his face was turned away and had tears welled up in his eyes.

"Many people get this disease, all different types. They treat it for a few months to make it disappear. In this case, your bump is too large to be operated on. The doctors need to shrink it with medication."

He asked, "Do you think I got this bump when I fell at the basketball game?"

My brain started to sizzle, especially since Ewing's Sarcoma can be triggered by an injury. I quoted what the doctor had told me, Although there isn't clear evidence, an injury may draw attention to a bone cancer that is already there.

I told Nicky the issues were not as big as it truly was. I wanted to tell him in small doses, as opposed to all at once. My god, he was a teenager, starting his first year of high school!

He said, "Mom, we've got this."

"We've got this together, Nicky," I echoed, as I stared into his big beautiful eyes.

I knew my son better than anyone. My instinct told me that when he said, "Mom, we've got this," it was his way of knowing he was about to grow up very quickly, gaining the strength to become a little man.

∞

NICK WAS SO in tune with himself and possessed a level of self-awareness that most kids his age didn't. Nicky was always a deep thinker. Our connection was unique. His Life Path numerology number is 33, which explains our deep connection. My Life Path is 11. It was so easy being his mother. His presence relieved me of my own painful childhood memories. This was my time to shine as a mother, to give it *all* I had.

The Life Path numbers 11 and 33 are considered master numbers in numerology. However, both 11 and 33 tend to internalize feelings. They keep them bottled up for the sake of harmony as they dislike confrontation. In essence, the relationship part of the chart reveals sensitivity, faithfulness, selflessness, intuitiveness, self-sacrifice, devotion, loving, and we possess the ability as a team to balance understanding.

The Life Path number thirty-three points to a powerful urge to care and protect, to shelter those you love and comfort them. This is where we were both very much alike. I can remember, in 2003, when my lights were turned off. Nicky walked down to the local video store and applied for a job. This was in his second year of his treatments. I saw the application on his dresser and asked him, "Nicky, what are you doing?"

He said, "Mom I want to be able to help you by getting a job."

He touched me so deeply with that gesture. I replied, "Nicky, that isn't necessary. We're okay. We'll be okay."

When I turned to walk out of the room, I quietly told Nicky I'd be right back and that I needed some things from the store. I drove up the Hutchinson Parkway crying so much my eyes felt they'd pop right out of my head. The thought that a fifteen-year-old child, sick with cancer, would think about helping his family was hard to take. As I drove, the song "Close to You" came on the radio. It was a reminder from the Universe of how close to my heart he always was and always will be.

We were totally connected.

That was more overwhelming as each day went by.

In that first week, Nicky was digesting and absorbing the news. He knew cancer was a bad word, but I'm not sure how much more he knew about it then.

The next day, Saturday morning, Nicky was still on the couch from having his friends over the night before. I had walked into the living room to pick up some glasses and to start cleaning the house, and I asked, "Want anything to drink?"

Again, he was lying on the couch balled up, the pillow over his head. He always did that when he wanted to hide away from the world. I curled up next to him and held him tight. I could feel his sadness and wished I had a magic wand.

"Nicky," I said, "This is going to be okay. We're going to get through this together."

He twisted towards me and asked, "Why did God do this to me?"

How do you answer a question like that from a child? How could I possibly come up with the words to comfort him?

"Nicky, God puts obstacles in our lives that we're forced to overcome, in order to move on with our journey. He's not punishing you, and it's not because you're a bad person."

"But Mom, I'm only fifteen. I won't be able to go to school."

"Nicky, you'll be able to go," I reassured. "We'll make sure you can go to school as much as possible. We're going to go on Monday. They'll give you medicine to shrink it down. That's our goal, and that's what we're going to do… And we're going to do it *together*, one day at a time."

∞

AS A REASSURANCE to myself, I called my friend Gianna before the weekend was over. We'd met during a fundraiser on behalf of the Montefiore Children's Hospital at the Polo Club in Connecticut. I had immediately embraced her sincere personality.

I lightly mentioned during our conversation that Nicky had been diagnosed with bone cancer.

Gianna's voice cracked, "Michele, I'm so sorry for your baby!" She went on and on explaining and offering up her magnificent and positive encouragement.

Trying to stay strong, I broke down. "Gianna, I'm so unsure and confused," I confessed. "The Montefiore wing isn't fully completed yet. Should I even think about having them see him there?"

But she put my mind at ease.

"Take him to NYU on Monday," she responded. "They have fantastic doctors. And professors. They'll do everything possible to heal your baby."

I trusted her advice impeccably.

∞

ON MONDAY, WE reported to NYU as scheduled. On this day, we truly learned what the next year would hold.

Even though I had tried to shelter Nicky, he knew it was big— he could sense it. My son always had a strong intuition about what was really going on. I had no real idea that he understood fully, but *somehow*, Nicky knew.

TEN

ALWAYS A SMILE

DURING THE SUMMER of 1993, the children were five and six. For my ex-husband's fortieth birthday, I surprised him with a month-long family trip to Italy. I wanted the kids to experience where their father's side of the family had come from. I was always very excited to explore life and show my children how life should be enjoyed.

While the trip itself was fantastic, when we returned home, everything resumed to normal, including our constant disagreements. It takes two people for a loving relationship to flourish, and the daily turmoil and pain I experienced cut as deep as that of a death. We had a lot of marital problems. Through a lot of self-help and discovery, I saw that the health of our relationship was beyond repair.

I needed out. I couldn't handle the uncertainty. I felt betrayed. All the broken pieces of our never-had-been love, I came to realize, laid shattered into a million pieces in my hands. And no amount of glue could put it back together. My reality was constantly shaken, and my children were caught in between. I knew for the sake of my childrens' perception of love, family, honesty, and security, which was my sole focus, I had to take charge of my own respect and dignity. My kids' emotional, spiritual, and mental behavior was my responsibility, no matter what the surrounding outside influences.

It didn't affect Nicky. He was smarter than that. He loved his father and could see beyond the surface, and he simply would not subscribe to it.

Nicky and I were alike in many ways. Instinctively, he knew to separate from the divorce. He didn't allow it to affect him emotionally.

∞

WHEN I WAS a child my environment was negative. I didn't want this same environment for my children. I made a plan to live close enough, yet far enough away after I acquired full custody.

The decision of full custody was unusual. However, looking at the circumstances, I was awarded full custody based on the evidence presented through their legal guardian.

Once the custody was in place, it would be the beginning of our journey together as "The Three Musketeers."

Immediately after the divorce, the judge allowed us to move within a three-hour distance from their father. I chose Westchester, NY, from upstate because, having grown up in the Albany area myself, I knew how limited the possibilities there would be for my children. And I wanted so much more for them. Moreover, I could see how they both had such individual and talented personalities.

My gut instinct told me I had to make a new life for us.

When we first moved down to Westchester, Nicky was very shy. At first, I drove him to school until he felt ready to take the bus. Being the new kid in town, he was worried about being teased or bullied. I remember the first time he climbed on that enormous yellow school bus for third grade. He looked so small, yet ready to embark on a new adventure. The bus pulled away and rolled down the street as tears rolled down my cheeks. It was the beginning of a new chapter in my son's life.

It wasn't long before Nicky had made new friends. He had a way of drawing people to him with his wonderful spirit, generous nature, and beautiful smile.

∞

BASKETBALL BECAME A big part of his life, starting when he was eight. His friend, Sho, who lived just up the street, embraced Nicky on his first day of school. As a mother, my first impression of Sho was that he was a young, creative Asian boy who gravitated toward Nicky's energy. He made my son's entry into his new existence smoother than it could have been. Nicky spent most of his time at Sho's house. In fact, he was there almost every day after school.

I later met Sho's brother, Ken, who had a great love for basketball just like Nicky. Ken also shared similar drawing and cartooning interests with Nick. They enjoyed drawing funny cartoons, and they both had a *wicked* sense of humor.

Nicky also loved football, ice hockey, and later on, he even learned to ski and play golf with me. We were a small family now. The three of us took weekend ski trips to Vermont and often passed through to visit my mother. It seemed that moving had been the perfect thing for us. That is, before Nicky became ill.

Since I was very much alone growing up without a sibling, my intention was always to have more than one child, so they could grow up together and be there for one another. And, I guess I was fortunate to have that dream even for the short time Nicky was in my life.

The three of us also loved to take road trips together. Spontaneously, I would pack a bag and say, "Let's go! We're off to see the wizard!" I'd never tell them where we were going because I wanted them to feel like each trip was a fairy-tale adventure. Bianca always ran straight into her room and threw her things into a plastic bag, not even stopping to pack. They loved to explore with me because it felt like a treasure hunt each time.

Another time, I took Nicky and his sister to Salem for Halloween with a stopover in Boston. They were maybe five and six. I wanted my children to experience an authentic New England lobster dinner with me. When the time came to eat the lobster, the looks on my children's faces were priceless, to say the least. Such a strange item there on their plates. A thing that was only known from the storybook, *The Five Chinese Brothers*. Both of them told me, "No way! Ma, no way am I eating that *big* lobster!"

Ironically, later on, during Nicky's chemo treatments, Nicky ended up loving lobster. He was always so hungry during his treatments.

Nicky also had a passion for sketching and drawing, and he would often doodle during class. His funny cartoon drawings always made us laugh because, although he wasn't a perfect illustrator, he tried. Ironically, my father, a successful businessman, was also an artist. I presume he had a genetic artistic influence on Nicky. My dad painted and sent me beautiful poems throughout the years, and I shared them with my children.

Looking back, I realize that perhaps Nicky doodled because he was bored with school, and he possibly wanted to explore more of life. To this day, I still have several of Nicky's drawings. I often wonder if maybe he was subconsciously aware of his spiritual connection to his grandfather (also a Life Path 11) as well as the Universe, and, perhaps, even his ultimate fate at a very young age.

∞

AT FIRST, NICKY'S teachers presumed he had Attention Deficit Disorder (ADD). They wanted to put him on Ritalin, but I refused to fill the prescription. I believe some children are just special, and some teachers are not aware of these gifts. They simply shrug it off, calling it ADD or some other nonsense.

I feel that every child learns in a different way. My child wasn't stimulated by his teachers nor by the activities during school, but they didn't want to hear that. Furthermore, I felt that the Special

Education team in the school didn't try to address his lack of attention.

Nicky always found it hard to pay attention. He was smart but not interested in sitting in a classroom. I could relate to that because I couldn't tolerate schoolwhen I was young, either. I found it boring. Like Nicky, my creative mind always ran on a constant fast-forward. And during his consistent weekly homeschooling time after the diagnosis, Nicky learned so much more from his teachers who *came to him*. Classroom learning was *definitely not* an option during those four years of chemo treatments.

∞

NICKY WAS ALSO a prankster. Halloween was his favorite holiday. He and his two friends, Ken and Sho, always did crazy stuff on the day, but the night before Halloween was their traditional outing.

Mischief Night, also known as Devil's Night, is a very Northeast U.S. term used to describe tricks and pranks the kids play the night before Halloween. It's an evening when people traditionally participated in harmless mischief. I stress *harmless* or *innocent* mischief because other forms of mischief can lead to big trouble.

My favorite memory is watching his old videos he made with his friends. His friend John had shoveled his car out from the snow so it would be ready for the next day's work. However, the boys re-buried it, *but* they covered it in toilet paper first!

Innocent and fun times is how I remember Nicky.

His favorite jokes were played mostly on his sister to try to get a rise out of her. On this one particular weekend, Nicky and Bianca had a sleepover with their friends. He decided to draw a mustache on her face with permanent marker. The next morning, she woke up extra early and walked to the gas station for snacks. She had no idea until the cashier told her how much he loved her face design.

Aside from Halloween, all holidays held a special place in Nicky's existence. He felt a sense of loyalty to spend time with those he held in high regard, in both friendships *and* family. Nicky was an inspiration to all of us. Our small family believed sharing love with one another was important, especially Nicky. He inspired us. In fact, we learned from him about his depth of loyalty toward everyone in his circle.

The family gatherings, no matter the size or location, were always out of the love that we shared with each other. Distance never affected or changed his feelings. Nicky always made every effort to see his father and grandmother upstate during these occasions. Even when the news we had gotten turned into the rigors of chemo, no matter how Nicky felt, he'd take the train in between his treatments to visit upstate as often as he could.

∞

MY MOTHER AND I didn't always see eye to eye, but when a family member is sick, true love should bond, no matter what. So, it was unusual and wonderful that my mother was so devoted to her grandson. Every other weekend, she would travel downstate and be there for Nicky, and, surprisingly, for me, as well.

Nicky was very religious from an early age. My mother was dutiful to her church, especially after her retirement. She attended twice a day, seven days a week assisting the parish, partaking in running errands, and helping the staff. Being a part of a Catholic-focused family is one thing I always encouraged during our quiet times alone in the hospital.

I prayed daily with Nicky, and, as he requested, I read Bible stories to him. It brought a sense of peace and calm to both of us. These were just small signs I picked up on knowing Nicky was preparing to return home.

While it had become my immediate family's practice to attend church only on major holidays, we frequently visited a special Grotto in The Bronx at St. Lucy's, much like Lourdes that stands to this day. Nicky had a collection of statues of the saints, which he kept in his room. He always touched them and played with them and looked at them, ever since he was little. I think he had a deeper connection to those things than most children. Mature beyond his years—he was an old soul, for sure.

∞

WHEN THE POPE died in 2003, Nicky was really upset. He made a shrine in his closet of his statues, surrounded by cards and letters that were sent from people from our church. Every week, they would send holy water over to the house, which Nicky drank each day, faithfully.

It had always been Nicky's desire to try a backpacking trip to Rome to visit the Holy places. He loved Europe and its different cultures, having been to Italy and France. He'd learned about the countries, about their history and different cultural ways. The two of us had a lot in common that way. After watching the movie, *The Way*, in 2010, with Martin Sheen and Emilio Estevez, I could imagine a pilgrimage walk through the Camino, an ancient spiritual trail to St. James in Galicia, Spain, in honor of my son. Having been to the Pyrenees in France with Nicky, I felt the connection in combination with grief for my son. We'd planned to travel to new destinations and, ultimately, the world together.

∞

IN THE HOSPITAL, months before he passed, Nicky grew a beard. When the nurses asked him why, he stated, "Because I want to go out like Jesus."

That was my son's spirit—he always had a smile for everyone, and he never lost his sense of humor. His warmth, love, and charm showed even during his toughest times.

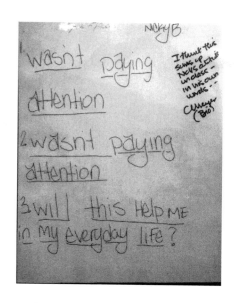

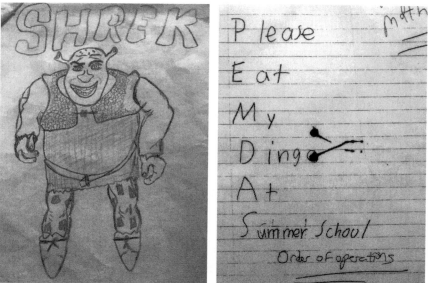

School was not his favorite. Creative expression is in the genes.

Don King

Harry PotHead

By Dick Bell

Michael Jackson

ELEVEN

RED DEVIL

AFTER NICKY HAD been diagnosed, we'd returned home. Word of his diagnosis spread quickly. Within hours, an outpouring of love and concern came knocking on our door. The line stretched from our front door and around the block. Nicky's friends surrounded him. The support shocked me. I knew he had lots of friends, but I never expected to see them lined up the way they did at our front door—all of them patiently waiting their turn to come inside and comfort Nicky.

When dealing with something internally as scary as cancer, along with its gruesome realities, we often feel alone in the world. But we realize we are not, as evidenced by the love and support shown by Nicky's friends—so the opposite is the truth.

∞

AFTER A LONG weekend, we returned to Manhattan on Monday to meet with Dr. Rausen for the first time. It was the beginning of a long and arduous journey.

I remember Dr. Rausen coming into the room and introducing himself. He was a tall, older gentleman, wearing round-rimmed glasses. He seemed to have a very gentle manner, I noted, as he introduced himself and we shook hands. My intuition had led me to believe that my son was going to be well taken care of. As I looked around, the nurses were so attentive and on target with the families and other patients.

We then walked across the street to NYU, where they would perform the procedure and begin Nicky's treatment. We checked in at admissions and were immediately taken up to the ninth floor.

This is where we'd spend the next four years.

"I want to talk to you about the procedure we're going to do," Dr. Rausen said. He explained they were going to place what he called "pig ears" inside Nicky's chest, so he could get intravenous chemotherapy to shrink the tumor. He said it would be a simple operation. Though he was very straightforward and to the point, I felt he didn't go into much detail, but seemed to make Nicky feel at ease.

While my mother and I waited, the doctor ordered several body scans, CAT scans, and x-rays prior to the "ears" procedure. After several hours, Dr. Rausen joined my mother and me in the waiting area.

He told us that cancer had apparently spread over the summer. Nicky's scans now showed tumors on both lungs. He said the cancer was at stage three.

The staging and grading system for cancer, known as the TNM Classification of Malignant Tumors (TNM), labels the stage of cancer, allowing the doctors to indicate the size and location of tumors, along with whether cancer has spread to any other organs. They use a 0 to IV scale to communicate size and invasiveness. Staging also helps oncologists and doctors decide which treatment options are best (e.g., chemotherapy, radiation, surgery, or combinations of the three). It signals whether the tumor cells appear abnormal and are likely to spread.

"Nicky," Dr. Rausen explained gently, "the treatments given could last up to three years," but honestly and directly. I was absolutely speechless and utterly frightened of the unknown regarding what could transpire throughout the years ahead.

Dr. Rausen said there were only six types of treatment, depending on what stage the Ewing's Sarcoma was at. In a calm voice, he explained every procedure that we would follow, reassuring me, "One thing at a time, one step at a time."

My burning question freely flowed out. "Dr. Rausen," I said, lowering my head in tears, "How long do we have?"

He said, "It could be one year, maybe up to three years, Miss Bell. We'll do everything we can for Nicky." Mom put her hand on her forehead and keened loudly, an I felt all my energy drain from me, like a vessel emptying, butter melting, an out of body experience of being hollowed out from within.

I didn't take Dr. Rausen at his word. I thought, *That* may be your prognosis, but I'm going to save my son's life. It's not going to happen to Nicky and me. I'm going to find a way to prolong his life.

And I often thought, over the next few years, that Nicky would recover. I was determined, as his mother, to keep his spirit alive.

My mother and I went to see Nicky in his room before his "pig ear" procedure began. I didn't share Dr. Rausen's three-year prognosis with my son, nor did I tell him his cancer had spread to his lungs.

A few moments later, the nurses came to place Nicky on the gurney and take him away. For the first time, Nicky witnessed the painful tears rolling down my face.

Nicky said, "It's okay to cry, Ma. I'll be okay. Don't worry."

I didn't utter a word. I just stared at him as though I would never see him again. I was beyond scared, and my body was shaking. The strength of Nicky's voice made me choke. This was my only son, the *very* son I had prayed to have for nine months. The unknown journey was about to begin.

I assured him, as did the nurses, as we rolled down to the elevator, holding hands, "Nicky, sweetheart, Mommy loves you so much," while I squeezed his hand.

Unsurprisingly, his humor sprouted, "Ma, if you keep squeezing, I might need a cast."

My hands released, holding them up to my face, trying to hide my utter sadness.

Nicky had the operation that afternoon, and he started chemo the next day.

∞

THEY USED A colloquial term for the first year of treatment. They called it the "red devil" because it's the most potent treatment you can have for aggressive cancer. It consisted of a three-drug regimen of Adriamycin, Cytoxan, and Doxorubicin.

Nicky's treatments lasted up to eight hours at a time. He was in the hospital for five days. During this time, he mostly slept, and he couldn't eat the entire week until we got home.

I slept at the hospital every night, and I left early in the morning to take the train from Grand Central to my workplace in Tuckahoe. My daughter slept at a friend's house. Our lives altered so quickly and abruptly. Mostly, I felt an emptiness inside. After work, I would run home, get some work clothes, and make sure Lily, our dog, was safe and being taken care of by the dogsitter.

I was filled with sadness for my son as I watched him lying listlessly in a hospital bed, his body pumped full of toxins.

Nicky was so drugged up from these "red devil cocktails" that he mostly slept during the week of chemo. He didn't even want to watch TV that first week. He just wanted to sleep through it all.

We never used the word "chemo" because it made Nicky want to vomit. I creatively came up with the word "cocktail." In time, specific chemo cocktails acquired special names. For instance, the more potent one, called "the Red Devil" was renamed to "Long Island Ice Tea." His menu of treatments was used as a mind trick to avoid negative thought processes when going through each treatment.

Following these intense treatments, we'd leave the hospital and immediately eat at one of his favorite restaurants. At this point, he was starving and would fill his tummy with either pasta or seafood. He loved Italian food and lobster.

The pattern was one week of chemo, two weeks home. Nicky had a large appetite because of the steroids and other medications. The community came together when they heard about Nicky. Mezzaluna in Scarsdale graciously offered meals throughout the years when our family struggled. These are the pay-it-forward moments we were forever grateful for. That's another reason why I'm confident I made the right choice in moving my family downstate. We would have never had the outreach where I grew up. I felt people had a whole different mindset there. I even experience this today, five years upstate, into caring for Barbara. Not many are here in the same way for her, though.

We found a wonderful nurse's aide, Elisa, who came to the house daily when Nicky was home. A huge inspiration, she loved Nicky very much. Today, Elisa remains a friend who never fails to send me wishes every holiday, every year.

Nicky would go out with his friends if he felt okay. But, mostly, his friends would come and sit with him to keep him company. Sometimes he'd push himself to go out with them. He didn't want to let cancer control his life.

I'd arranged for him to be home-schooled and also for Elisa to come care for him while I worked. His "pig ears" needed to be cleaned and bandaged, and Nicky needed extensive monitoring to avoid any further complications, such as infections or anemia.

When Nicky was home during those first two weeks after his treatment, he often needed a platelet transfusion. His red blood cells had to be at a certain level for the next round of chemo. We would drive to the Hassenfeld clinic every other day, just for a finger prick.

After a full week of chemo, plus the testing and transfusions, the process seemed endless. But the transfusions enabled Nicky to build up his immune system for another round of treatments. Driving back and forth on the FDR, the daunting daily trips seemed hopeless at times. There was always bumper-to-bumper NYC traffic. As I drove, in my peripheral vision, I'd watch Nicky sleep for the entire ride.

If he got a transfusion, we would have to stay at the clinic the whole day, or at least eight hours. The first three years of treatments were given in the hospital, one week on, two weeks off. It was important that Nicky clear his system of the evil toxins running through his body, so I researched types of water to help him come home earlier than predicted. Penta was the winner. There were no impurities found in that water, plus it was free of pesticides. Penta was ideal for Nicky's optimal hydration throughout the remaining years. I ordered three cases a week. I felt the water's higher Ph level of 9.5 flushed out the chemo from his system and allowed him to return home more energized than ever.

We could spend time at the clinic, or I could give my son more time together, and that was the choice I made. Before going home, we had to make sure he was filled with enough fluids, and once home, he drank three to four tall bottles each time. Without this intervention, his levels after chemo might have kept him at the hospital for more hours. Our motto became, "Drink up, and let's get the hell home."

∞

DURING THE FALL, Nicky lost weight, and his skin color and physical appearance drastically changed.

One day, during the last week in January 2003, he said to me, "Ma, watch this." Then he pulled out a big chunk of his thick dark brown hair. This was a massive shift in his condition, and Nicky was very affected by it.

The next morning, leaving the hospital to get to work by nine a.m., my mind was scrambling. How could I continue working while Nicky was alone at NYU those early afternoons with no one to hold his bucket when he got sick? Who would rub his back?

That morning, my assistant Renee had placed my coffee and buttered bagel on my desk. I walked over to her, leaned on her desk, and asked, "How am I going to ask Gary for time off so I can be with Nicky?"

Renee suggested I call Gary to perhaps leave early and work from the hospital. After a few hours, I gathered up the nerve to call. He wasn't available immediately, so I left a voicemail. Later that afternoon, he called back. "Gary," I said, my voice shaking, "my son has been alone at the hospital during his chemo treatments for the last four months. Is there a possible solution where I could arrange to leave work two hours early each day and work from the hospital?"

He was stern in his answer. "I'll get back to you."

With Nicky's hair falling out, I needed to spend time with him. I didn't see any reason why I would be denied being with my son—or was there?

I'd been hired as a real estate specialist at an affluent apartment complex in Tuckahoe, NY. My job performance remained stable. I arrived every day on time, and always stayed until the end of the day, even when my son was alone in the hospital for two weeks each month during his morning treatments being injected with the Red Devil.

After Nicky started his first round of treatments, I continued to travel back and forth to the hospital. I needed to be with him during the afternoons because he was on a lot of medications for combating his nausea. I wanted to be there to comfort him and hold the bucket after his treatments for him to throw up. Between his diagnosis, when I started the job, and by the end of January, I missed a total of four and half days of work. It was so important that I be with Nicky, yet I was confronted with much future stress.

∞

ON THE FOLLOWING Monday afternoon, Gary called me into the conference room. With the building superintendent present, he told me, in a very abrupt and businesslike way that I was, in not so many words, *fired*.

"We no longer need you here at the building," he stated bluntly.

He didn't give a reason, and he didn't mention Nicky. But I knew why he was doing this because there was no other reason. I'd been a good employee who was never reprimanded for anything.

I asked, "Why are you doing this? I need my job. I'm a single mother. I'm the only one supporting my children."

My boss shook his head. "We don't need your help in the building."

Stunned, I headed back to my office to get my things. I could hardly think straight. *What was I going to do?* My boss and the building superintendent stood outside my door, waiting to escort me out of the building.

I had the job for only six months, trying to get my life in order. I moved, numb, hurt, in tears as they led me out the door. *How were we going to survive through Nicky's illness?* My assistant Renee watched—she was very supportive—and she's still my friend today. She couldn't believe what they were doing.

Immediately, I hopped on the train to see Nicky. I showed up just after noon before his treatment.

∞

SEEING ME AT midday, Nicky asked, "Mom, why are you here so early?"

I gently said, "Because I wanted to be with you." Although this was true, I didn't have the heart to tell him why I had really finished work so early.

"Are you sure?" he asked, almost as if he already knew the answer to his own question.

"Yes, Nicky. Everything is going to be okay," I tried to reassure him.

He looked at me and knew. "You lost your job because of me, didn't you?"

I didn't know what to say. I couldn't explain to him what had happened, but he knew something was off. "No, Nicky, not *because* of you. I'm taking some time off to be *with* you. Don't worry. We're going to get through this."

∞

AFTER FOUR MONTHS, the tumor that was wrapped around his fibula had shrunk so much, it was now possible for the doctors to go in and remove it. Nicky had his first surgery on February 14, Valentine's Day 2002. It was our favorite holiday together.

After the surgery, Nicky needed to wear a leg brace because some nerves had been hit during surgery, causing a drop foot. Even though I felt concerned about him not being able to walk straight, his walking situation seemed like *nothing* compared to my thinking that the cancer had been removed from Nicky's body.

At this point, I was totally convinced my son would recover.

∞

WITHIN WEEKS AFTER the dismissal, my supervisor at Tuckahoe tried to look into my termination but got nowhere with the company. I had no idea the Federal Family and Medical Leave Act requires businesses with fifty or more employees to provide unpaid time off to care for sick relatives.

Even the mayor of Tuckahoe, NY, the town in which we lived, thought my situation was a shame. He told *The Journal News*, our local newspaper, "Sometimes you have to have a heart, especially when a situation involves a child with cancer."

∞

AFTER LOSING MY job in the third week of February 2002, I now had no income and only a small unemployment check. Our health insurance cost ran $800 a month. We were not eligible for Medicaid. The trips to the hospital were very expensive between parking, gas, and tolls. Luckily, after we showed the receipts, our social worker at the hospital arranged for us to receive a monthly stipend from cancer societies to assist with these expenses. After nine months, we had to move from our home into a small apartment.

I spent my quiet time, while Nicky was in the hospital, writing to attorneys throughout New York, New Jersey, and Connecticut, seeking representation. The attorneys would have their paralegals mediate for them, and not one attorney offered to discuss the termination.

One Sunday afternoon at NYU, Nicky was resting, so I decided to move to the other side of the room and watch the Lifetime Channel. I started watching a movie inspired by true events, called *A Child's Wish*.

I couldn't believe the parallels between this movie and our life. Similar to Nicky's story, her injury led to a sarcoma diagnosis. Missy had been kicked in the thigh while playing soccer. Her father, played by John Ritter in the movie, was *also* fired from his job after asking for time off. Just like me.

The most intriguing part to me was Missy's selfless "Make-A-Wish" request. She wanted to meet Bill Clinton at the Oval Office. Without Missy's wish, I would have never known about the FMLA law.

Unfortunately, the company I was working for did not meet this employee number, or so I was told. Until I found out later, the developer owned several satellite companies, which totaled well over that cap employee number. 50 was the magic number of employees. You would think that my employer would agree with the spirit of the law, even if he wasn't legally required to allow me time off, but that wasn't the case.

Who would think that a dozen years later, I would be telling you this next anecdote?

Talking for many pages about the devastation of cancer can drag any reader to despair, however I want you to know another part of Nicky's long story. In the summer of 2015, I was browsing the IMDb website to search out more details on "A Child's Wish" for this book. I was determined to find Missy's family. They deserved to know the grateful impact their little Missy left on our family. Just below the page was a space to leave a review, so, of course, my curiosity led me to keep digging.

While reading the reviews, I felt drawn to one in particular. Tiffany Moya. She'd written on July 6, 2006:

I attended 6th grade with Melissa Weaver, and I remember the day I found out she had died. I think it may have been a Monday, and the announcements came on saying that anyone wanting to attend Melissa's funeral would be excused from classes. It was over 10 years ago so I may have forgotten details. But one thing I will never forget is the feeling I had when I found out someone so young... My age! ...had died.

We had all known that she had cancer, she always had the cutest hats, but one ever really thought she would die... Death was a word that wasn't a part of our life. After Melissa passed away, her mother (a teacher) set up the gym with things from Melissa's life such as her hats and letters and pictures... She talked to the school as a whole and helped us understand what she had gone through. It was an experience I shall never forget. Although I wasn't a friend of Melissa's (we never had classes together), it made me very sad that someone so young could leave us like that.

*ALWAYS IN MEMORY OF MELISSA WEAVER,
YOUR FELLOW CLASSMATE… TIFFANY.*

As I read Tiffany's review, all I could think was how she, and her post review was lead to me. These are the tiny miracles you ponder, and wonder how did this happen?

*"Miracles don't always manifest themselves as a major cure
or a financial gain. They come in small pieces and often
discreetly, where no one ever sees that the miracle happened.
But they come, indeed."*

Nine long years had passed since her posting. And here, all these years later, I wondered to myself, *would it be possible that one day I could meet the Weaver family?*

That afternoon, I wrote a short note to Tiffany. In the subject line, I put "A Child's Wish" ~ Melissa Weaver.

I won't post the entire message, but basically, I wrote:

'I read your review on IMDb, which is how I found you. If you ever get this message, although you wrote it nine years ago, will you please email me?

I, too, lost a child to cancer, without going into too much detail. This connection is really important to me. If it is meant to be, I will hear from you.

Many thanks, Michele

Six months later, at five a.m., I woke up to look at my messages. Tiffany had written back. I could not believe my eyes.

Tears started to fill my morning eyes. Closing them gently I crossed my hands onto my chest. Another grateful moment has come my way. My morning meditation intention, simply grateful.

It had been a rough week for me with my mom, her Dementia was progressing, and so this wonderful news superseded all my sadness.

We exchanged phone numbers and social media info. It was an immediate, intimate connection between the both of us. I explained our story briefly in text, mostly because my insides were twisting with excitement. She has no idea what I was about to share was coincidentally Melissa and Nicky's exact same stories.

It was a serendipitous moment.

I needed time to marinate what was going through my head, how moved I was that the universe could bless me this way. It took a few days of processing it all. It took me a few more days to work up the courage to call her. I needed to just sit with the joy of it all.

It was surreal enough for me that I got on my hands and knees in front of my son's Pieta, wrapping my arms around all I have left of his memory.

Everything happens for a reason. You trust, pray and trust again that the higher power in which you believe is truly watching over you. In my case, my prayers were answered.

After one year of searching for an attorney for being wrongfully dismissed from my employment, I found the help we needed.

But now back to Nicky's journey...

One year into being injected with the Red Devil and the first surgery on his fibula, Nicky was eligible for a Make-A-Wish. In December of 2003, the three of us went on a cruise paid for by the Make-A-Wish Foundation. On this trip, we met the Ferraris, who welcomed us as though we were family. This was my first experience in learning that there are people in the world who care besides one's immediate family.

During our Make-A-Wish cruise, at our table for breakfast, lunch, and dinner, our assigned friends were the Ferrari family. It was a beautiful scene, with us all sitting together at each meal. I knew Nicky was taking it all in, enjoying every moment. Luca and Vera, traveling on a holiday vacation along with their three beautiful daughters, plus Uncle Al, Luca's brother, who was in a wheelchair, sitting across from us. The second night into our cruise after dinner, Luca asked me to take a walk. Both Luca and Uncle Al escorted me to the upper deck.

From his chair, Uncle Al looked up and asked, "Michele, what's going on with Nicky?" I shared our tragic story that led us to our holiday cruise. Observing Uncle Al with one arm and one leg, I was humble in my approach as I did not want to feel we wanted any sympathy.

Luca continued, gently, with his right hand on my shoulder, smoking his cigar, "If you need anything, just ask."

I looked up and said, "Thank you, Luca."

He was deeply sincere, and I felt relieved. I later had spoke in detail about our situation in the lounge, including the struggles and my job loss.

My focus was to enjoy every moment away from the medical world, but I couldn't help but elaborate on that Make-A-Wish trip, on the deck of that ship. I explained about being fired after asking for ten hours off a week. During our conversation, Luca promised me that, when he returned to Florida, he'd have his lawyer contact me to take care of the circumstances with the New York City developer.

After we disembarked from the cruise, the Ferrari family invited us to come stay at their home. I naturally said yes, so the three musketeers set for another adventure! Bianca, even grumpy at first, got to spend more time with me and the three Ferrari girls, creating a girl-clique all their own.

Within a week after returning to New York, Luca's lawyer contacted me as promised, and we met.

Eventually, I received my lost wages. That helped me to pay the rent, the medical expenses, and give Nicky a quality life in his remaining years. The Universe places people in our path when we need them the most.

To the Ferrari family and attorney—you have my gratitude, always.

Ferrari Family we met on Make-A-Wish cruise

TUCKAHOE

Woman's firing draws ire of local officials

Single mother's son has cancer; No legal protection is found

Bill Hughes
The Journal News

Four days after she began a new job as a leasing specialist at an apartment complex in November, Michelle Balduzano had for 14-year-old son, Nick, had bone cancer. The bump on his right leg just below his knee was caused by a rare disease known as Ewing's Sarcoma, which occurs most frequently in teenagers.

Bell, a single mother raising her son and a teen-age daughter with no child support from her ex-husband, struggled to balance her new job with the demands of her son's medical treatment, which included several sessions of chemotherapy, blood transfusions and surgery.

By her count, she missed two full days of work and five half days from her job at the Riverview apartment complex on the border of Tuckahoe and Yonkers near the Bronx River Parkway over the past three months. On Feb. 5, Bell said, her supervisor called her into his office and told her she was being to go. Bell said she was given no reason.

"I was so devastated, I can't even describe how badly I felt," said Bell, her voice cracking with emotion. "The worst part is that my son, on top of everything else that's happened to him, had to ask me if it was his fault."

Bell worked for Manhattan developer Trevor Davis, whose Riva Development ventures and leases the $2-unit apartment complex and refinancing assistance to facility for senior citizens. Her supervisor, Gerry Swords, referred calls to a company spokesperson.

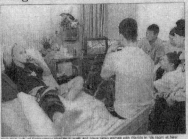

Nick Bell, left, of Eastchester shares a laugh and plays video games with friends in his room at New York University Medical Center in New York City.

Nick Bell with his mom, Michelle of Eastchester, in his room at New York University Medical Center. Nick is suffering from Ewing's sarcoma and is recovering from surgery and went to remove a tumor from his right fibula.

SPOTLIGHT

Bell bounces back from battle with cancer

By Danny Laprione

TWELVE

A TALE OF TWO CITIES

LTHOUGH THE YEARS have quickly accumulated since Nicky's passing, I've come to learn many things in the aftermath. Some things I couldn't have grasped at the time, as I was so busy taking care of my immediate concerns of being a single mom, two children, a deadly illness. and an unknown outcome. My head is more focused now to revisit the things that were, at the time, important to my son and daughter.

One thing, in particular, was watching my son grow into a man beyond his age. I had wondered what influences brought him to such manhood at such an early age since his father was not prominent in his life. At the time, I wasn't aware of Nicky's father's cultural influences. But, in 2015, nearly ten years after Nicky's passing, I was invited to a preview of *A Bronx Tale: The Musical*. As the story unfolded before me, I was overwhelmed by how much my son must have absorbed from the story. I do remember him talking about the film, but because he was sick, I couldn't focus on what he was saying.

It appears that *A Bronx Tale,* the movie, was a powerful influence on Nicky. He didn't see it as a gangster movie, but rather as a morality tale. Also, the lead character, Sonny Lospecchio, became his father figure. It is often said, "Art reflects life." In this particular case, it couldn't have been any truer. When I sat down in 2015 and watched *A Bronx Tale* from beginning to end—live on stage as a musical—I discovered many of the things that Nicky would discuss with me while he was alive. Things that then I couldn't grasp at the time because I was so focused on his health.

Looking back, I realize that, as he grew into a man, he had become very particular in his dress, appearance, mannerisms, and character. All items that resonated within this film. Like the young boy portrayed in the movie, Nicky was drawing whatever lessons he could from his real dad and the character, Sonny, in the film. The parallels have become quite profound for me.

My son was always a respectful young man and admired by many. He adopted several of the deeper meanings of this story insomuch as how to treat people. As an example, Nicky said to me one day, "Ma, what if I dated a black girl?" I answered, "Whatever makes you happy, Nicky." A little smile came across his face.

So, he clearly took all the positive messages from *A Bronx Tale*. As far as I am concerned, for an eighteen-year-old man to see beyond the surface of that film was astounding. Therefore, this chapter, A Tale of Two Cities, is basically, The Bronx meets NYC—my son discovering the deep meanings of the film.

My son's bourgeoning Bronx character meets his nemesis of the NYC Red Devil.

Nicky's treatments were administered on the ninth floor of the NYU hospital. On each visit there, he brought his own DVDs. I would always see *A Bronx Tale* in his selections. When you are doing chemo, you have nothing but time. Yet, deep down, Nicky knew this was his most valuable time, and he chose to spend it watching this film. I can now fully understand, as it's a wonderful morality tale, and I've come to understand the lessons he gleaned from watching it so many times. If he fell asleep during the movie and woke up, he would restart it from the beginning.

Nicky was even well aware of the character, Sonny's, lack of faith in people. Yet, as the young boy Calogero in the film had faith, so did my son. Although I don't want to say my son modeled himself after a film character, he did connect with the deeper lessons and also with the character's psyche. Nicky could see all that at such a tender young age.

The young boy in *A Bronx Tale* wore a chain with a cross around his neck. It made much sense then that, on Nicky's sixteenth birthday, he was insistent on wearing one of the same chains. Nicky wore that cross proudly, and when he passed on, I laid it across the pieta. A "pieta" is a statue of the Blessed Mother Mary and Jesus... Nicky's ashes are kept in the urn's bottom. Nicky saw to the left while other kids saw to the right. They saw a tough guy gangster movie and my son saw spirituality, not to waste talent, unconditional love, and to be fair to all. The movie is really about family, values, and choices.

To this day, it still astounds me, my son's observations of life, that he could see things I couldn't even see myself at the time. I guess you could say Nicky taught me then, and he continues to be my life teacher, even today. It's easy for me to keep his memory alive because I truly believe he was an old soul and, therefore, he had so much to teach everyone. He still had much to give yet didn't have the opportunity to give it. His time might have been up, but not his life's work. It's not only a great loss for me but a great loss for all those who knew Nicky and could have learned from him.

Nicky even started his own social club in the garage. It was called the Boom Boom Room. In a way, he became The Don, of sorts, to all his friends. They looked up to him, respected him, and it was astounding to watch from a mother's point of view. His friends never left his side. They would spend countless hours, days, and weeks in his company.

Music would blast above the garage in the Boom Boom Room. There was also a lot of loud laughter. I suppose you could say, the typical sound of young boys and girls having a good time. As I walked up the driveway one day, I heard them emulating the dice game scene from *A Bronx Tale*. Each of his friends playing a different character in the scene. All I could hear was them singing, "Stick 'em in the bathroom" at the top of their lungs.

Today, those same red dice he played with are next to me as I write this book, and I look at them each day for inspiration.

I witnessed my son growing into a man highly regarded by his peers. At home, he'd always think of me first, my well-being, and if I needed anything, like if I wanted to go out to eat. He would suggest first, "Ma, let's take a ride down to Angelina's tonight. Gianni Russo is singing your favorite classics."

Before spending the night out with his friends, Nicky was mindful of how a young man treats his mother.

And he tapped into knowing what I liked—J Lo perfume for Christmas, roses for Valentine's Day or a day at the racetrack. We enjoyed one another's presence immensely.

I didn't fully understand it then, but it is clear to me now—what an amazing, wonderful and productive leader my son was destined to be. To this day, his friends still reach out to me. They tell me how much they miss his presence and how he influenced them into their current careers.

One friend of Nicky's that comes to my mind is Danielle. At twenty years old, having known my son, she became a nurse, an RN. That's a huge accomplishment at such a young age. She wrote these words to me on his ten-year anniversary:

"This day, ten whole years ago, this Earth lost a very special and unique individual. Although my time with him personally was much shorter than many others who loved and adored him, he indeed made an irreplaceable mark in my life and spirit. It is because of this person I chose the profession of nursing.

"I was in my first semester of nursing school when Nicky transitioned, and it was through him I pressed on through all of its difficulties, as hard as it was. Most

people know I became a nurse at a very young age. I have dealt with many types of situations in my career that doesn't come easy to your average twenty-year-old.

"In tough times, during my professional career, I've thought of Nick and his courage, faith, and perseverance through his most difficult times as an adolescent. And then I think to myself, HE dealt with things more difficult than that of your average teenager. I've watched him at his best, and I've seen him at his worst. I've watched him suffer through all the side effects of chemo, and I saw how much it drained him.

"And I also watched him keep his humor and personality through it all. I've also seen him on his best days, making others laugh or laughing with other people, simply enjoying the happiest parts of life.

"To this very day, I have never met a stronger individual in my life than he. And, as much as I wish he were still here to this very day, making me laugh for hours on end, I know that he was called for a reason: to watch down on us all. I am ever so thankful to have had him as a friend. And I am forever grateful that he has touched my life."

People these days seem to think that today's generation is all about entitlement, and they are frivolous in their desires in life. However, through my son and his friends, I see it as a fallacy. Young people today are just as intelligent, feeling, and thoughtful as anyone else who walks the earth.

Through my son, I have learned to expect the unexpected. I have also learned never to give up, to see people for who they are, and accept all because those very same people, more often than not, will surprise you.

Cancer may have been mutating inside him, but his mind was so busy that he had no time to think about the next day's cancer drama while he was entertained through the art of film.

Nicky was a man of hope, not negativity. Reflecting again on the movie, *A Bronx Tale*, this was a story of hope for the future and the carrying on of the next generation, and for that, I am thankful.

Despite what may have come our way when we walked through the doors of death, through our long, arduous drives up and down the Bronx River Parkway into NYC, which lasted at least an hour, we lived the tale of these two cities for four and a half years.

As a parent, one cannot imagine the feeling of fighting a long battle you may not win, but that's how it was.

Danielle Vespertino and Nick at Casino night

THIRTEEN

TRYIN' TO STAY STRONG

NICKY ENJOYED LISTENING to all genres of music and mixing CDs with his new mixer. A friend of mine who worked as a DJ for 103.5 FM came over to show him how to use his new DJ equipment. Music kept Nicky on-course and focused. He listened to his own CD mixes as he faced those Red Devil treatments or while I drove him to the city. One day, driving home after six hours of chemo, we were in traffic when he broke out singing "Close to You" by The Carpenters.

I looked over at Nicky, holding back tears. We sang the song as a duet. Truly like a scene from a movie. These are the little moments that will stay with me forever—the moments I'm ever so grateful for, yet I miss terribly. It was a message straight from his heart to mine. One of the few ways he could do it, sensitive as he knew I was. Our communication levels went deep.

Being faithful and religious, Nicky knew he had no control over anything—control belonged to God. He was trying to make a bad situation bearable, which was one of the similarities we shared.

One afternoon, returning home from lunch with his friends, he left a certain song in our car's CD player, ready to listen once we started. Knowing I was next in line to drive, he set up a certain song that moved something deep within me. The lyrics in the song nearly crushed my heart. The song was "Throwback" by USHER.

I'm goin' out of my mind and I'm runnin' out of time
I'm trynna stay strong I don't wanna crack
Lose some then I lose again, when am I gunna win some?
I just want things to go back how they used to be
You never miss something 'till it's gone
That's my word ma, you convinced me
It might not happen, but I'm still hopin'
And my heart is broken, but the door is still open

The words felt pretty intense, and I knew it was Nicky's message to me. If you like, I suggest looking this song up online. I think you will enjoy hearing the message Nicky was giving to me. He was a deep thinker, and the lyrics in some of these songs are what got him through each day.

There were times it would take us an hour to drive to the city in morning traffic. Nicky listened to Howard Stern. My mother would be in the car, but Nicky didn't care.

She would complain, "Nicky, that man is filthy."

And to lighten up the moment, Nicky would reply, "You love it, Gram." He knew his grandmother was no angel, as we all have moments of disobedience. "You know you love it, Gram."

Without my push or encouragement, Nicky—on his own—wouldn't have been strong enough. The two of us holding each other up with unconditional love is what got us through, though.

∞

TRYING TO SURVIVE childhood cancer was the same arduous routine every day, week after week, month after month—year after year—non-stop and never-ending. Hospitals give many people feelings of anxiety, including myself. Here we were, approaching the smiling secretary as we arrived, before signing in and waiting hours for the doctor to see us.

The daily trips for a finger prick to the clinic in between chemotherapy were daunting. Making sure his blood and platelet levels were pumped up for the next round was the goal. *Our* goal was to get out of the clinic as soon as possible. We loved seeing Dr. Rausen and his staff, but we didn't look forward to ending up there for eight hours to get transfusions if the levels were low.

Dr. Rausen and his caring staff became our family for five years. Some days, I would get so annoyed waiting for the blood or platelet runs from the hospital. The days were always filled with unexpected obstacles. That is where my conversations with God would become pronounced, at the clinic, inside the bathroom on my knees, having a moment, begging and bartering for my son's life.

One of the hardest parts was constantly seeing the other kids who waited with us at the Hassenfeld clinic. It broke my heart as I always saw the sadness on their faces. I didn't know what to do or what to say to them. Each child and their parent(s) was on their own journey of facing sickness. And often, that sadness seemed reflected on the faces of each parent.

My eyes teared up often as I tried to send a smile across the room to the mom who seemed distraught. Sitting quietly, I held my son as he played on his phone. Time spent for me looking around the room at other parents, taking in all their emotions. It consumed my heart, but I tried to save my energy to keep Nicky going. I was emotionally drained every day as I had no outlet except food.

I'd always try to comfort a parent if I saw them in distress. Once at the hospital, I approached a mother whom I hadn't seen on the ninth floor before. I knew she was at the beginning of a long, or maybe short journey through hell. She looked so confused.

I asked gently, "Is everyone okay?"

She began to talk about her son. He had suffered a relapse.

She confided, "We live in Florida and will only be treated by Dr. Rausen."

At that moment, I was reassured we were in a good place. I had heard only good things about this doctor since our initial onboarding. It was a good day for me, and it came because I was willing to comfort someone else.

∞

AFTER NICKY'S OPERATION on Valentine's Day, and throughout the following months, Nicky grew frail, skinny, and extremely tired. He'd lost so much weight, and he didn't have the strength to go back to school. But all that changed after the one-year anniversary of the Red Devil treatments.

After everything Nicky had endured, he was beginning to look good again, and he was even gaining weight. I believed the heavy-duty chemo treatments could work. I began to think the cancer was gone from his lungs for good!

Cancer devastates a family financially, as well as emotionally. I had lost my job because of taking so much time off to care for Nicky. There was never enough time to spread between Bianca and Nicky. How does any parent? We had lost one home and then another. We moved from NY to CT and back again. We traveled long distances for chemotherapy and surgeries. I couldn't ask my mother for financial assistance as she would insist we move back to our family home, and Nicky's father wasn't in a position to be supportive.

What was a single mom to do?

Friends were caring and helpful. I thank the heavens that various cancer societies provided us with transportation assistance during treatments. Without that help, and that of the local individuals in our community, Nicky's short time on this earth would not have been so blessed.

Then, in April 2003, Dr. Rausen ordered another bone and body scan and found the tumors in Nicky's lungs *weren't* shrinking.

At this point, I felt helpless. I thought maybe we should get a different doctor. I felt helpless. I couldn't take the pain away from my son. I had been hoping and praying for a miracle, but now, I felt defeated. I turned to my faith to keep going.

∞

OUT OF THE five to six tumors they'd found, Dr. Rausen told me that only four of the smaller ones could be removed. Surgery was scheduled on Nicky's right lung. My son stayed ever the optimist.

Arriving at the hospital, we met with Dr. Rausen to discuss the procedure. He comforted Nicky immensely, describing what he was about to be doing. He gave Nicky dignity as a young man.

I helped Nicky get his hospital garb on and his hat. I took a picture of him with a big smile on his face just before he went into surgery. The surgery lasted five hours. This was his first lung surgery to remove as many tumors as possible.

Mom and I sat in the waiting area for about three hours in soft, comfortable chairs. We took turns visiting the chapel and praying all of those tumors would be removed. I was filled with optimism and making deals with God to save Nicky. My mother's anxiety made me very nervous when she kept asking me questions for which I had no answers. Like I was some sort of all-knowing fairy! I would stare at her as she rambled on, hoping for encouraging words of comfort or maybe a hug. I felt so lost.

Dr. Rausen came out of the surgery room in his hospital scrubs. "Ms. Bell, is Nicky's father not here?"

I stood up from the chair next to my mom. "No, doctor, he was unable to make the drive."

He proceeded to explain. "I could only remove four of the six on his right lung at this time. He'll be in ICU for the rest of today."

When I heard the news, my heart sank. I realized I was going to faint. So I sat down. Dr. Rausen reassured us that the remaining smaller ones should shrink with the next round of Nicky's chemotherapy.

I had honestly hoped they would be able to get all of them out. I guess I was too optimistic. Isn't that what every parent is supposed to be—hopeful—for their child's disease to be cured or to disappear?

The last thing you want is to see the expression on your child's face when you break the news to them. And if the truth needed to be told, sometimes we leave out the really bad details—until it's absolutely necessary.

After finding out the results of the surgery, I gravitated toward Nicky. He was lying in his bed, and I moved closer, soon wrapping my arms around his waist. A world of mother's comfort on his hospital bed. The beeping of the machine that gave him oxygen made a steady and strong sound there in the ICU. I spoke to God often, begging Him to help me find the words to soothe Nicky when he woke.

Nearby, I heard my mother come up behind me. She nervously started whipping the curtains back and forth, a *subtle* way of getting Nicky awake.

Nicky woke up, and for the first time ever, I heard a curse from him. I hoped then, through his anesthesia, he heard me asking her, "Be still. Quiet." With his eyes open, he appeared hopeful, in spite of the curtains, still fighting every challenge coming his way.

As I sat there and stared at this innocent life that had so much to live for, tears flowed. I reached for his warm hands while he slept with my head pressed gently against his shoulder. I remember hearing his groggy voice as he asked me to play the theme song to Rocky on his iPhone.

When he had fully awoken, he seemed very strong, wanting to know how the surgery had gone. *How would I tell him they hadn't been able to remove everything? How would he handle hearing the news?* I couldn't imagine what it would feel like to hear what I needed to tell him. That wasn't even the problem. I just wanted to be strong for him. However, sometimes that was difficult to achieve.

∞

THERE WERE TIMES when I struggled each day in the hospital, not knowing what the future would bring if I couldn't make ends meet for us. But somehow, I managed to carve a niche with my real estate skills. During my daily hospital visits, where I used to stay occasionally overnight, I worked from my computer. And not one of my clients knew what was going on in our lives. I learned how to work when Nicky was asleep in the hospital or with friends once we got home.

A few months before Nicky transitioned—allow me this term, and you may use any term you can speak, in your own circumstances.

So, when Nicky was at home in hospice, three weeks before he transitioned, I was again running low on funds. Even turning to family was stressful. Christmas was weeks away, I was behind on paying important bills, and I needed to come up with the other half of my rent. There *was* a commission due, but it was a month away in coming to us.

I kept plugging away to close transactions. My career as a hair and makeup artist was on standby since I couldn't commit my time, in case I had to be with Nicky at some point. Real estate kept us afloat for the remaining years, and I could juggle my schedule better to care for my terminally ill child.

I never wanted to leave his side, for those unexpected illnesses kept cropping up, such as colds, fevers, chills, earache or a headache, blood disorders, anemia, and so on. To this day, I don't know how I managed, but I kept my emotions tightly in check.

Before beginning a career in real estate, I felt a calling to help others. Feeling inspired, I started the charity Skipper's Angel Wings. It took eight months to complete all of the paperwork. Usually, this task is done by an attorney. However, I did it all by myself during the days I spent in the hospital with Nicky. On my days at home, I cooked for Meals on Wheels and the hospital staff. I felt like I had a purpose.

> *Sometimes it is important to stop and look how far you*
> *have come on your road to understanding and peace.*
> *We are not the same people we were in those first awful*
> *hours of loss—we've cried, we've fallen—but we've*

> *also grown to understand that real treasure can only be found after we have searched for it. We have come so far, and although there is more road ahead, each of us can see the glimmer of light as it comes closer with each passing day.*
>
> *Take a moment today to reflect on how much you have learned, how much you have accomplished, and how far you have come. We may not see it clearly now, but legions of loved ones are proud beyond measure of our small steps toward hope.*

I wanted to make a difference in the lives of others who were facing the same emotional and financial rollercoaster challenges we faced. The only way I knew how to do this was from my own experience.

My mission was to help provide assistance to *any* family with a child who had been diagnosed with cancer. Once the charity was set up, we held our first fundraiser: a Bachelor/Bachelorette auction. We packed the house at Sweet Caroline's restaurant in Eastchester with some of the finest and generous single men and women from all over Westchester and NYC. The turnout was fantastic with the help of Mike Padernacht, owner of Sweet Caroline's. He was the top prizewinner of the auction when his admirer paid $1,000 for a date! Nicky, fifteen years old at the time, drew the next largest bid of $800.

Guest comedian Goumba Johnny donated his time to host both of our events. Nicolette Minozzi, one of the attendees, joined her girlfriends, who contributed to her winning "Frank the Fireman" for a $600 bid. Nicolette, one of the bachelorette bidders, told news reporters when she saw the story about the auction, she wanted to be involved because it was a great cause.

Following this successful event, we were able to assist families in need. We raised a little more than $5,000, which helped alleviate the financial burdens of thirteen families in the New York region.

My motto was: "No family should endure financial struggles when their child has been diagnosed with cancer."

I felt inspired to hold another fundraiser with Louis DiCarro Salon hosting a casino night. Local businesses donated gifts for the silent auction. These added donations went towards helping even more families, which helped subsidize rent, non-healthcare bills, food, clothing and/or transportation costs to nine more families.

My one candle wish was to gain enough momentum in forming a stable board to be able to buy land to build a getaway camp in Upper Westchester County with therapy horses, live animals, and activities. Unfortunately, I was unable to continue this organization on my own. Hopefully, one day this wish will come true, and I'll be able to help more terminally ill children fighting cancer.

I knew I wasn't alone in fighting these battles. There were many of us faced with the same plight. Even when I could help even *one* family, I was determined to make a difference.

Aside from the financial strain, the continual emotional strain also never let up. Part of the problem came down to the fact that my family and his father's family were both so out of touch with the reality of my son's diagnosis.

∞

I KEPT FAMILY and friends informed, but I don't believe they truly understood the arduous daily routine and long hours involved in Nicky's constant treatments and care. We never knew what crisis or challenge would present itself next.

Constant worry about the cancer spreading was only *one* of my concerns. Then there was the toll all the treatment took on Nicky. Chemo drained him so much—to the point of me wanting to cry for him every day.

"I always hoped a new era would be born to embrace mindfulness."

I tried to explain to people, paternal family members most of all, but the connections between emotional and physical strain never hit home. All they understood was that my son had cancer. But, beyond that, they seemed to be in denial about how that cancer was slowly taking Nicky's life.

In a way, I don't blame them. It's one thing to hear about it, and quite another to live it and watch it, hour by hour.

Anyone who has had cancer or been a loved one's caretaker knows as soon as you hear the word CANCER, it takes over your entire life. All routines are broken, and new ones must be established.

∞

THE TUMORS CONTINUED to grow. We then received news that they were traveling to Nicky's other lung, so he underwent another lung surgery one year later, in May 2004.

Throughout this ordeal, Dr. Rausen never made it seem like a tragedy. He kept talking about, "…shrinking the tumors, and then doing lung surgery again."

Because he had been put on steroids, Nicky went up and down in weight. He lost a lot during that first year of chemo, but during the next year or two, he gained some due to the steroids. And his hair regrew after the first year. It wasn't as thick as it had been before, but it grew again because the later chemo treatments lessened in intensity.

Nicky was vain about his appearance, especially when he was not feeling well. He would stay at home if he felt he looked sick. He didn't want his friends to see him that way. Perhaps, he thought, they would feel he wasn't getting any better, and he didn't want to disappoint them.

∞

SO, RIGHT FROM the beginning, from beginning of his diagnosis, I decided to homeschool. His friends always called to check in on him, and they often wanted to come and see him. They would visit him at NYU frequently to watch TV together and play video games in his hospital room. He was blessed to have so many friends.

He maintained a good social life. He would even get on the train to go and visit his father's family in upstate NY for the holidays. I encouraged anything Nicky wanted to do socially, especially when it came to staying in contact with family members on both sides.

At this stage of his journey, Nicky felt upbeat. Even his doctor had been optimistic. I felt it, too. I never wanted Nicky to lose hope. I wanted him to live every day to the fullest.

∞

I REMEMBER DRIVING down the FDR parkway on the east side of Manhattan one afternoon to get some clothes and to find some solitude from the constant rush in the hospital. As I was driving, I felt overwhelmed and started sweating. Then I couldn't catch my breath.

Looking onto the East River Greenway and driving under the tunnel at Sutton Place, my anxiety increased so much, I swiftly exited East 53rd. I pulled over onto 2nd Ave and sat in my car watching everyone go about their day.

I heard nothing around me. I just saw the motion of people's daily lives, wondering if they were facing good times or hard times. I broke down behind the wheel and screamed so loud, it hurt my throat.

After that scream, my son's pain and suffering became a reality. Everything I had been pushing against came to a head. It had all burrowed deep into my soul. I prayed to my grandmother for strength.

I was shaking inside and couldn't control the thoughts running through my head. I admitted myself to an emergency room, and they gave me anxiety medication to calm me down.

After filling the prescription, I had to return to my son. Once I arrived, Nicky asked, "What took you so long?"

I explained that I needed to have some quiet time at home. Then he said, "Mom, *I'm* your quiet time. Please don't worry. We're going to be okay. Just believe."

Now that I was beginning to feel hope again, I wanted to take Nicky away for his birthday in June. We set off to St. Martin.

My son possessed such a remarkable sense of humor—and this only continued to grow stronger. He celebrated the good days and brightened everyone's days.

∞

LIKE I MENTIONED once, with his pranks and his friends, nothing kept Nicky from trying to be an ordinary kid. Here's more on his favorite pranks.

One winter, after a big snowstorm, Nicky and his friends decided to play a prank on his friend John. It took them a while, but when they were done, they had moved all the snow that John had shoveled off back into place! John's car was under a tall, deep mound. They recorded the entire prank on video.

Another time, Nicky filled a condom and then left it in the freezer. I'm not sure where he got the darn thing—I never even thought to ask—but can you imagine my surprise when he asked, "Ma, get me an ice-cube, please," innocent as anything. I went to the freezer and found his surprise.

When I turned around, Nicky was standing there, grinning from ear to ear, and then he burst out laughing. I picked up the flaccid, not yet frozen condom and tossed it at him. He caught it, laughed with me, gave me a kiss on my forehead, my third eye. And then left with his buddies for a night out on the town. Nicky always kissed me goodbye no matter where he was, and whenever I woke up or came home.

FOURTEEN

HOPE, MIRACLES, AND HEALING

I HEARD THAT thousands of sick people traveled to Lourdes, France, every year for hope, miracles, and healing. Let me tell you about 2004 when, in spite of everything going on in my life with Nicky, and to my surprise, my mother offered to take Nicky on a pilgrimage.

Without hesitation, I agreed—relinquishing my son for the trip, I said *yes*.

Nicky was filled with excitement, but he was also searching for a cure. I dreamt that when he returned for his next scan, he would be free of this disease.

While I received many calls from Nicky during his stay in France, I'll never forget one in particular.

He told me, "I want to come back here next year. But it has to be with you, Mom," he said how much it would mean to him if we visited Lourdes together.

"Nicky," I said, "I'd do anything for you. Yes, we'll arrange a visit together."

And so we did. In a grace, Marlene Watkins was privileged to be the leader of the group, Our Lady of Lourdes Hospitality North American Volunteers, the first Lourdes Hospitality outside of Europe. Nicky wanted me to come to Lourdes (he asked Marlene while there—that is an extraordinary story in itself!).

Nicky couldn't wait for me to visit this holy place because he knew how much I loved Europe. He hoped to receive a blessing to cure his cancer. Our hearts were as one in this regard.

At my request, as a non-profit charity and Lourdes Hospitality, they wrote a letter to the Knights of Columbus in Eastchester to help sponsor my pilgrimage costs. Again, Marlene was privileged to be the leader of that group when Nicky was 17 years old— we were in Lourdes altogether! Marlene told me once through an email, "Michele, I will never forget you, your mother and your extraordinary son, Nicky Bell"!

We boarded our Air France plane at JFK, and we were off. Arriving in Paris, we found our way toward the Pyrenees terrain.

We awoke early in the morning with a view of Château Fort of Lourdes. We needed to grab breakfast before our long day ahead of us. Nicky wanted to take me to McDonald's to get an Egg McMuffin and a beer. Yes, I said beer. But I chose a cappuccino, instead.

As we walked to the Basilica and drank the holy water, I recognized how strong Nicky's faith was, and his will to survive was such an inspiration to me. I had always held him in awe. My son had it so together at such a young age. During our visit, we attended daily mass together and explored the city.

When my mother felt a little too much anxiety, her sarcasm would inadvertently aim at me. Times like these, Nicky would gently say to his Gram, "God is watching you, so behave and be nice to Mommy. She knows what she's doing!" Nicky was always a calming influence and very protective of my sensitive emotions.

While in Lourdes, Marlene personally asked MSGR. (Bishop) Perrier to exceptionally grant permission for Nicky for the Sacrament of Confirmation at Lourdes (it is exceptional because it is a Sanctuary/Shrine and not a parish). As documentation, she requested (kindly insisted) the letter be written. They arranged for Nicky to be confirmed in Le Cachot, the humble childhood home of Bernadette Soubirous, by Fr. Tadeusz Rudnick, a Ukrainian bi-ritual priest, which is allowable because of my mother's heritage.

Although I requested from our local church, time was of the essence as many of his friends back home had attended confirmation classes to receive the most important sacrament in his religious life, Nicky was unable to due to his treatments, transfusions, and surgeries.

The story told of Bernadette captured Nicky's imagination, she who was promised happiness, not in this lifetime, but in the next one. She too had something like he did. She too was a teen with something in common beyond their twin-strength and belief—their illness.

The number of pilgrims visiting there each year reached nearly a half-million. And we three joined them on our own journey for a miracle. The highlight of our trip was the baths. The story goes that on a Thursday afternoon, February 25 in 1858, the Virgin Mary said to Bernadette, "Go drink at the spring and wash yourself in the waters."

The line at the baths could take hours, and Nicky went each day, standing in line with his leg in its brace.

The men and women have a separate entrance to the baths—each has seventeen bathtubs, all made of marble and filled with the water of Lourdes. We were taken privately into the changing room and asked to remove all our clothes. Then we were each wrapped in a sheet and guided by two volunteers who immersed our entire bodies into the bath.

Upon our release from the bathwater, we found ourselves *completely* dry. I asked Nicky, "Were you dry too?" As we were guided away toward the confession, we were asked by the *hospitaliers* (the French term for religious order members who cared for the sick and needy) to present our petitions, make the sign of the cross, and to pray freely to Our Lady of Lourdes and Saint Bernadette.

The experience was breathtaking and heartwarming.

On our last day, we decided to do something fun and daring. We visited Le Pic du Jer, a mountain summit which sits within Hautes-Pyrénées, overlooking Lourdes, Tarbes, and Pau.

Obviously, the views from all of these sites are spectacular. We all rode the Funiculaire, a century-old railway that connects Lourdes to Le Pic du Jer. The ride was beautiful and only took about six minutes to travel up the one-kilometer distance to the top. I have a phobia of heights, so I sat on the floor of the Funiculaire. There is a café at the top. Nicky and I explored the trails while Babsie (our nickname for my mom) grabbed a beer.

Our trip felt short, but it was consumed with prayer. Our mornings were inspired by the view of a beautiful castle outside our window. We began each day with a walk into town for breakfast.

We later walked through the village to the Basilica while capturing the slow-paced theme, which we both very much enjoyed. As we approached our group, we walked in an entirely different direction toward the Lourdes hills arm-in-arm, as we explored.

Nicky's presence filled every moment with inspiration, me holding his hand, never wanting to let go.

When we held hands and bonded as mother and son, I wondered if anyone who didn't know us could understand. In Europe, holding hands is a common gesture of friendship or love. Often, people said we looked like a couple, and Nicky would blush.

∞

SECRETLY, I HOPED and prayed I would see my son as someone's husband and father one day with a beautiful family of his own. I knew someday I would need to share my son with a lucky lady.

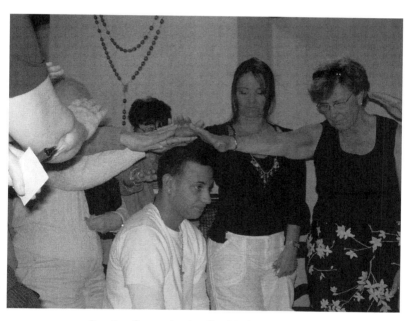

Praying for a miracle after Nick received his
final sacrament in Lourdes, France

Outside of St. Bernadette's home as a child

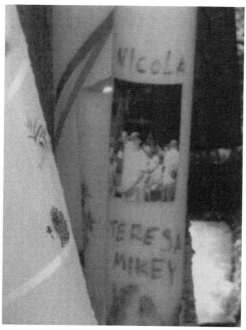

Nick sets pray intention for himself, cousin Teresa and friend Mikey

SANCTUAIRES NOTRE-DAME DE
LOURDES

Lourdes, May 25ᵗʰ 2005

Rev. Pastor
Saint Augustine Parish
115ᵗʰ Street
North-Troy N. Y 12182
USA

Father,

This letter is to inform you that Nicola Frederick Mele-Bell, at his request and with the permission of Mgr Jacques Perrier, bishop of Tarbes and Lourdes has received the sacraments of Confirmation and of the Sick here at the Shrine, on May 19, 2005.
Nicolas is the son of Nicola P. Mele and of Michel Bell. He was born on June 20ᵗʰ 1987.
and baptized in your Parish.

Father Tadeusz Rudnik celebrated the sacrament of Confirmation at the Cachot, here at the Shrine of our Lady of Lourdes. His godmother of Confirmation is Barbara Feyl.

The motive for this special celebration was Frederick's physical health. He is very sick with terminal cancer. He was accompanied here by a physician.

If you need more information, please feel free to contact me. This is my E-Mail: cjmduguay@yahoo.fr

Yours truly in Jesus and Mary,

ASSOCIATION DIOCESAINE
de TARBES et LOURDES
Sanctuaires Notre Dame de Lourdes
1 avenue Monseigneur Théas
65108 Lourdes cedex
LOURDES   N° Siret 389 017 101 00061

Fr. Marcel Emard Duguay, cjm
Chaplain, Our Lady of Lourdes
1 avenue Mgr Théas,
65108 Lourdes Cedex

Filling up his water bottles with holy water to take back home

FIFTEEN

'I'M DONE'

I N THE SPRING of 2004, two years into the chemo, I was driving Nicky to the Hassenfeld clinic for his treatment one afternoon. My mother came along that day, too. Nicky hopped out of the car first. The streets of NYC were full, and he and my mother went directly into the clinic while I took the car to park it. Or so I thought.

He must have gotten on the elevator without my mother and gone to a different floor. Or maybe he veered off to the deli. But my mother remembered which floor we needed to head to as she followed him, or at least, she thought she was following him. We all knew where the clinic was. It was the place we'd met Dr. Rausen when Nicky first was diagnosed.

I'd gone to park the car in a garage instead of dealing with street parking, which meant feeding the meters every hour with quarters. Thirty-Fourth Street is a very busy Manhattan street, and the clinic is right near the entrance to the Queensborough Bridge. I arrived on the tenth floor of the Hassenfeld clinic to find my mother frantically talking to the receptionist.

I asked, "Ma, what's the matter!"

"Nicky's gone! They can't find him anywhere!" she blurted, with much concern.

I replied in utter bewilderment, "That's impossible! He's gotta be here."

"He's *not* here! And he isn't answering his cell phone. They're gonna call the cops and start searching for him."

The receptionist assured me, "They call it a 'red alert,' for a missing child in the clinic."

This meant they would send out security to scour the building as they shut down elevators, lock doors, and secure each exit with a guard. In NYC, this a very serious situation since.

This time, it was not an amber alert—Nicky had taken off.

I tried very hard to keep my composure. I instinctively knew where Nicky might've gone. Even though he was full of good humor, all of these treatments and appointments were beginning to take a toll.

The long days of hospital treatment, the cocktails Nicky now received, were limited for his treatment and given at Hassenfeld clinic every day for two straight weeks. Driving in the NYC traffic did not allow us enough time for Nicky to vomit at least six times. We had prepared three buckets in the car and bottled water ready to clean them out. The chemo was tremendously powerful and made him extremely nauseous.

At sixteen now, he wanted and longed to be a regular kid again, and not a cancer patient. Nicky had expressed feelings about this to me on several occasions. My motherly instincts told me he had walked to Grand Central Station, got on a train, and had gone home.

I was right—a few hours later I did receive a text: *Mom. I'm home.*

We drove back to Westchester, traffic and everything. I walked into his room, and there Nicky was—all curled up on his bed.

I sat next to him and hugged him, saying, "Nicky, everything's gonna be okay. We're gonna get through this."

He shook his head, and his eyes welled with tears. He hadn't questioned his treatments too much at the beginning. He'd been very innocent and cooperative, and never asked how long it would take. But after two years of chemo, he felt defeated.

He didn't say why he left, but he didn't have to.

I said, "What do you wanna do? Talk to Mommy. If it's too stressful for you, we'll go away someplace. Let's go to St. Maarten. We need to get out of here. We'll deal with it when we come back."

I always tried to coax him out of his deep depressions with something that would make him feel better. I knew he loved St. Maarten, so I immediately went online to research flights. This was our escape from the raw reality of life or death. Protecting his soul from any more sadness was the ultimate medicine.

I felt I was barely surviving too—emotionally and financially. So I concentrated on trying anything I could to maintain my son's sanity.

∞

THIS DISEASE WAS now such a big part of our lives. I don't know how to describe it, except to say that I felt like I had cancer, too. In my own way, I felt Nicky's every pain, and I was willing to do anything to make that pain go away. It was like I could read his mind and feel what he felt, even though I hadn't personally ever truly experienced, first-hand, the depth of his disease and everything he was going through.

We were so bonded. In fact, Nicky felt more like a twin than my son. Two souls occupying the same space, experiencing a disease, each in our own way, yet I was unable to make any of it go away.

∞

IN 2004, after Nicky's first trip to Lourdes we planned a trip to the Mayo Clinic as I felt we needed a second opinion. I wanted to be sure I had tried everything I could to cure my son. First, I needed to get approval from Dr. Rausen.

With approval given, my mother, Nicky, and I flew to Minnesota. Marlene, our new friend from Our Lady of Lourdes Hospitality North American Volunteers was again, instrumental and arranged per my request for me to take Nicky to Mayo Clinic through one of their doctors.

These genuine gestures gave me peace of mind that I had done all I could—Marlene had attested in an email, after we re-connected through a group page on social media; a request for the letter from Lourdes be permitted for placement in our book, "Michele, there was medically no stone unturned or nothing you missed or didn't do for your beloved son"!

And it worked!

With our spirits lifted, we left our hotel for our appointment at the Mayo Clinic. The visit lasted an hour. They said that we should continue our treatments with Dr. Rausen. This was disappointing. I wanted them to say they had some miracle treatment to cure my son once and for all. Yet I felt relieved and blessed hearing Dr. Rausen *was* our best choice. I tried to make light of what we had just heard.

The last thing I wanted was for Nicky to sink into depression. He had such high hopes. But I knew he was disappointed too.

∞

I CONTINUED TO do research about Nicky's cancer, contacting lung doctors and lung organizations to see if it was possible to secure a donor. I even thought about offering one of *my* lungs to him. But I found lung transplants weren't common when it came to cancer patients. Then I started to realize—I was hiding the truth from Nicky. I had been hiding it from him for more than two years.

I never dreamed my son wouldn't stay with me. I thought we could do treatments for the rest of his life and keep his illness at bay forever.

When Nicky was seventeen, in March 2005, I received a text message from him telling me he was done with his treatments.

I texted back: What do you mean, you're done?

Nicky: I want to live my life as a normal teenager, and whatever will be, will be.

I didn't know what to think. Once again, I was devastated. I couldn't believe Nicky had made such a big decision. Cancer is such a rapid illness. I didn't know what to do.

I told him, "I'll support any decision you make. But the chemo's keeping the cancer in check."

"That's bullshit," he replied. "It's not going away. The tumors aren't getting smaller. I'm not going to live the rest of the life I have left in a hospital."

At this point, I realized Nicky knew his days were numbered.

I got on the computer and searched, yet again. I found a company in Texas that treated pediatric cancer patients with a glycol-nutritional supplement. You couldn't be on chemo during their treatment, however. That was the rule. No chemo. I was desperate for results, so I took out a loan to pay for the supplements.

By this point, I was grasping at anything. The supplements were extremely expensive, but I was adamant about Nicky taking them. Every time he came in the door, I told him, "Take one."

He wasn't too thrilled because he needed to take about forty-five supplements—fifteen capsules three times a day. He took them for about five weeks before his next full body scan.

Nicky often had full body PET scans after treatments for accurate imaging of the disease's progress. The scans also determined Nicky's chances of survival. It helped the doctor focus on choosing between surgery or some other treatment.

His PET scan was performed in a matter of minutes and involved scanning his heart, lung, kidneys, spine, liver, pancreas, gallbladder, thoracic aorta, abdominal aorta, adrenal glands, lymph nodes, spleen, and certain pelvic organs. In addition, this type of scan could diagnose cysts, aneurysms, and arthritis of the spine. It even told you whether you were at risk for the disease spreading further.

The day of the test, Nicky told me, "If this doesn't work, I'm not taking any other pills."

Later that afternoon, we learned that they had found even more tumors after the scan. Dr. Rausen responded to every detail we had questions about.

My desperation got me on the computer to research perhaps another non-invasive treatment. I came across TomoTherapy, the newest technology craze in the cancer world. It involved a beam of light directly targeting the tumors in every area of the body.

I wondered if Nicky had a chance to try this new technique on the newer tumors in his lungs, on the bigger ones? I wouldn't know if I didn't make the call. Thankfully, the office was close to our home and the only one in the Northeast area.

By now it was mid-April, 2005.

"Hello, my name is Michele Bell," I said to the receptionist over the phone. "My son, Nick, has remaining tumors on his lungs. I want to have him treated immediately with TomoTherapy. We have little time to wait since the tumors keep spreading. Will you please help us?"

She explained in order to get an appointment, they needed all of Nicky's records sent over.

∞

IN MID-APRIL 2005, Dr. Rausen offered Nicky more treatments, but he refused them.

They explained to me how sometimes this happens with cancer patients. "Maybe he will change his mind," Dr. Rausen said, "so try to be supportive."

Dr. Rausen was informed of my request for the TomoTherapy, and he supported—not my decision, but my determination as a mother to fight for her child's life. One month into the treatment, we had another PET scan with no results of shrinkage.

∞

I IMMEDIATELY STARTED to plan a very elaborate surprise party for Nicky. I made sure it would be a celebration not only of his birthday, but also of his life. I wanted the best for Nicky—the best invitations and the best wording on those invites. I knew that when Nicky turned eighteen on June 20, it would be his last birthday.

It included the best of everything. I invited all of his school friends, all of his relatives and close friends of the family. Dr. Rausen even took the train up from Manhattan.

The room was filled with all his friends. His father and both grandmothers came to his party and a few of his cousins. We had hoped to have all his family there, but I guess some of them were very busy.

I held his party at the VIP Club in New Rochelle, which was a total surprise to him. I had told Nicky a month or two earlier about a wedding I had to go to and asked him if he would be my *date*. My friend, MaryBeth, was the culprit in our plan to get him to the *wedding*. She would come over to visit us and show off a fake engagement ring, as we discussed her wedding plans.

His high school graduation year was nearing, where all of his friends would walk center stage to receive their high school diploma. I hoped the school would call me about Nicky graduating with his friends as he had been home schooled for the last four and half years of his life. My gut told me there would be no graduation diploma for Nicky, nor a courtesy call.

Still, I called the school each day leading up to his graduation, leaving messages with various school officials.

A week before graduation, I received a call from the Superintendent of Eastchester High School. They refused to honor Nicky on stage with a diploma or some sort of honorable achievement award, even after I begged on the phone.

"Let me ask you a question," I said, "would you allow the school not to give recognition if this was your child?" The phone went silent for a brief moment. His voice was stern as he elaborated it was not their school policy to give a child a diploma when they had not completed state requirements.

I felt utterly disgusted. Especially since their motto is *Earn, Learn, and Return.*

I was enraged by the ignorance and saddened about what was going through Nicky's head as he watched his friends receive their diplomas that afternoon in June 2005, just shy of six months of when he lost his battle to cancer. He was truly determined and diligent in attending his curriculums during both good and bad days.

In light of the choice the school had made, my son may not have been able to walk on stage that afternoon, yet his name WOULD be mentioned to the entire auditorium in between handing out diplomas.

I intended to make a sizable donation on behalf of Skipper's Angel Wings to the students in Special Education. The announcement came before all of the diploma announcements.

A person from the school announced this from us: "Nick Bell of Skipper's Angel Wings Children's Cancer Fund has made a donation to our Special Ed class students. Nicky has been fighting cancer for the last four years. While he has been unable to attend school, he has been home schooled to the best of his abilities. We are honored to accept this generous donation from Nick Bell & Skipper's Angel Wings."

After the speech, I walked out, leaving Nicky in the third row supporting his friends as they received their diplomas. I knew, deep down, that Nicky felt left out, and so when he came home after graduation, he seemed a little depressed.

I jumped off the couch, saying, "Nicky, let's go shopping for your new suit for the wedding. Maybe we can catch a Cirque Du Soleil show, too!"

We loved shopping together, so we decided to take a trip to Manhattan for the afternoon. We walked all over Midtown, in and out of any shops or boutiques that caught Nicky's eye.

We stopped in St. Patrick's Cathedral, as we both loved to light candles in this beautiful church. We walked for hours. Even though Nicky wore a brace daily because of his drop foot, nothing stopped him from moving forward.

Appreciating a full day without thinking about his disease, or about dealing with the hospital or his treatments, we absorbed the beauty of our time together. The vibrancy of the city life made us feel alive and motivated to face our fears. We ended up at Michael Kors for his suit, and Coach for his shoes.

Nicky's taste in clothes was exceptional. He had a classic style all his own, and he always made a statement. In the back of my mind, I knew that whatever he picked out would be the clothes he would be buried in.

That hot June afternoon, a week after his birthday, we were both getting ready for his party. I had to make sure we were running late so everyone would arrive before us. Nicky still had no idea what was going on.

At the VIP Club, I walked in first, and Nicky followed. Suddenly, everyone stood, screaming and shouting, "Happy Birthday!" His friends and family surrounded Nicky, giving him hugs and kisses. They played the music from *The Godfather* when we entered, one of his favorite movies. Nicky had always been about respect and loyalty.

When we were dining in restaurants, Nicky's hat would come off, and he would sit down only after I had sat. His unusual gestures were quite unique for a young man. He was a pure gentleman.

I always thanked my lucky stars when I saw him express his manners in public. I remembered him as a small child, and he would never get up and run around the restaurant after he finished eating. I didn't even have to tell him not to. He knew it wasn't polite and that it would've annoyed me.

At his party, we danced together to "A Song from Mama" by *Boyz II Men*. The lyrics to that song were perfect for that moment, too.

"You taught me everything and everything you've given me
Looking back when I was so afraid

- 115 -

And then you come to me
And say to me I can face anything
And no one else can do what you have done for me
You will always be the girl in my life.
Mama, I just want you to know I'll never go a day without my mama
Lovin' you is like food to my soul."

That was the first of our last dances together. With those lyrics, it was a celebration. Every little detail of the party came together for this special night. I made sure the balloons were black and silver because Nicky loved those colors. We put together a photomontage, made from pictures from when he was a baby, all the way up to the age of seventeen.

And we all danced around to all our favorite songs, including, "You and Me Against the World" by Helen Reddy.

Then, with Nicky by my side and looking at me, I read him aloud my birthday thoughts:

> *What a glorious day. Every face I see is a memory.*
> *It may not be a perfectly perfect memory. Sometimes*
> *we've had our ups and downs. But we're all together,*
> *and you're my son for a day. And I'm going to break*
> *precedent and tell you my one candle wish—that you*
> *would have a life as lucky as mine, where you can wake*
> *up one morning and say, 'I don't want anything more.'*
>
> *Eighteen years. Don't they go by in a blink?*
>
> *I wish for you that you will discover a woman who will*
> *love you and who is worthy of you. A woman who has*
> *grace, compassion, and fortitude to walk beside you as*
> *you make your way through this beautiful thing called*
> *life. I loved Nicky from the moment he was born,*
> *and I love him now and every minute and breath in*
> *between. And what I dream of today, Nicky, is that*
> *you will stop worrying about Mommy.*

*Our bond is unconditional. I want you to live life
every single day with no regrets, just as I have. Sing
with rapture and dance like a dervish, babe.*

Happy Birthday, Nicky. I love you.

After the cake, we all went outside with the balloons, including
Dr. Rausen. Nicky made another a wish, and then the entire party
released them over Long Island Sound.

Nobody had a clue that it would truly be his last birthday.

SIXTEEN

GOING HOME

NICKY SPENT THE rest of that summer enjoying time with his friends. He had a fun-filled few months that included going to Bermuda and spending weekends with his friends at the Jersey Shore. His routine *never* changed, and he never missed a beat. Nicky kept his moments moving forward beneath the exterior of his thoughts.

∞

ON HIS BIRTHDAY, he looked great. His transformation into a man was happening too quickly. Where was my little Skipper? My immense faith kept me hoping for a miracle to make the cancer go away. I never lost faith. I was sure that magic would remove this disease from my innocent boy, who'd always had a genuine belief in God.

Then, on August 8, 2005, at around one a.m., Nicky started yelling, "Mom, come in here." I'd gone to sleep early because I was having major surgery at New York Presbyterian at six a.m. It was unclear, but my potential prognosis was cancer of the uterus, so this surgery was imminent and important for my well-being and safety.

I could tell from the panic in his voice that something was wrong. With urgency, I ran to his room. "Nicky, what's wrong?"

"I can't get out of bed. There's something wrong. I can't move!"

The only question that came to mind was, *What should I do?* I was willing to do anything, but my mind had gone blank.

Then, I heard him say, "I want you to call Doctor Rausen. I can't walk!"

He hardly ever complained, and so I knew this was serious.

My mind raced as I called the doctor. He said, "Bring Nicky down immediately."

My mother had already driven down to come with me while I was having surgery, but instead of calling on her, I reached out to one of the mothers who had been so helpful during these unexpected struggles. She drove down and stayed with Nicky during the night, so I was able to have the surgery that morning.

I must say that if I hadn't had surgery, I would not have been physically able to take care of Nicky the last months of his life.

Just before my surgery, I called Nicky to let him know I was going to be okay. And once he was scanned, he would be too. He replied with, "You'll see me in your dreams. I love you, Mom."

At that point, they put him on morphine because he was in *a lot* of pain.

Later that afternoon, after my surgery, I called Dr. Rausen's nurse, who told me they did a bone scan, which showed tumors now growing on Nicky's lower spine. They were also advancing up to his neck. Dr. Rausen announced he wanted to do radiation immediately.

∞

SO, NOW NICKY was back in the hospital—the last place he really wanted to be. However, this time because of his circumstances with his lower spine, it wasn't like he could walk away. I secretly wished that he *could*. Even now, with the situation the way it was, we had always forged ahead with making plans for our future, like taking a cruise the following year followed with a backpacking trip through all of Europe.

Now, my wish in his honor is to walk the Saint James Way to Santiago, later sprinkling his ashes into the sea at the cliffs.

I don't know if I can explain this correctly because Nicky and I had never spent our time talking about his illness. We both knew we had to deal with it, so why talk about it? At the same time, Nicky knew that if he wanted to, I would certainly listen and talk about anything he wanted. Nicky just wanted it simple—enjoying our time together, no matter what the circumstances. Neither of us was in denial, we were just dealing with each day as it came.

So, talking about future cruises, or whatever else he wanted to talk about, was fine by me. It was so easy being his mother. We took pleasure in each other's company.

∞

AFTER HIS BONE scan, the news that I had been dreading finally arrived.

They were scheduling another round of chemo, and we listened as Dr. Rausen indicated the possibility of more surgery. When our conversation with Dr. Rausen was all said and done, one thing was certain—Nicky was going to be in the hospital for quite some time.

As soon as I could, after my surgery, I hopped in a cab outside of New York Presbyterian and went to NYU to see my son. As I approached the entranceway, there was a nurse's aide with a wheelchair. I was wheeled into the hospital and down the long hallway, then into the elevator. I felt like I was going to burst with excitement.

All the way to the ninth floor, I was talking about how I was going to surprise my son. How he had no idea I was coming and that I couldn't wait to squeeze him tightly and never let go.

The elevator door opened, and I was wheeled into Nicky's room.

To my surprise, he wasn't there. In that instant, all I could feel was complete fear.

"Oh my God. Where's my son?" I shrieked.

Then I heard, "Boo!" When I turned, there was Nicky—he had been wheeling his chair behind me *the whole time*. Somehow, he'd snuck up behind as I arrived at the hospital.

I was so happy to see him that I started crying. I didn't want to leave him and go home without him.

After a couple of days, they did release him. With the aid of a walker and cane, along with heavy-duty pain meds, he could walk now. Nicky went back to the hospital after a couple of weeks for more radiation. But for the rest of August and that September, he didn't want to go back, even though it was only one day a week.

∞

BY THE END of October 2005, Nicky's walking became worse. They put him on steroids and other medications. He continued to have radiation, but only in small doses in the spine and neck. He went through more bone scans, which showed that the radiation wasn't really helping. His walking continued to worsen—to the point that he really couldn't walk anymore. One day, Nicky got so angry, he threw his cane away and broke down crying.

"I can't believe this is happening to me. I'll never be able to walk again. I'll never be able to play basketball again," he revealed.

My emotions inside were on fire. I felt helpless watching him. I felt his pain in this condition, but I wouldn't allow myself to cry in front of my son. I had to remain strong. I could only hold him, hug him, and never let him think we were giving up.

I had another idea on how to brighten Nick's spirits. I contacted the publicist for Vida Guerra, an FHM swimsuit model that Nicky was in absolute awe over. Their model of the year in 2004.

He always used to say "Ma, she's gonna be my wife one day."

She would call him throughout his treatments. Vida could speak about only positive thoughts. While she was on set or shoots, they woud carry-on on the phone. Somehow, my son always got past the surface of things. I think deep down he had the power to strip even celebrity away and get to the real person, no matter who they were.

Looking straight into his eyes, I said, "Any woman would be the luckiest wife in the world, Nicky. Your devotion and love is priceless."

∞

A MONTH BEFORE he passed away, during our late-night talks, Nicky mentioned that he would never have his own family. He talked about being a basketball star or possibly a coach, how he wanted to travel the world and find the woman of his dreams. To get married and have a big family. As a child, my dream was to be the best mother possible, guide my children through *their* dreams, and explore life way outside the box.

We were *so* much alike.

At the end of October, Nicky went into the hospital again.

During this time, a very close friend, Mikey, whom Nicky had befriended over the years during previous hospital stays, was dying from the very same cancer—Ewing's Sarcoma— just a few rooms down from where Nicky was being treated.

Mikey's beginning story was eerily similar: He' been hit in the elbow, just prior to noticing something was wrong. And, as mentioned earlier, Ewing's Sarcoma is usually triggered by an injury.

Mikey was an African-American kid, and Nicky called him, "My brother-from-another-mother." Mikey, an adopted kid from Brooklyn, was a very kind young man. I noticed he would always be alone at the hospital, which made me sad, so we'd "adopted" him into our own family. During those four years, he would come to our home in Westchester and spend days with Nicky when he wasn't having chemo. With Bianca upstate with her father so much, Nicky was lucky enough to have a new *sibling*.

They could just be kids together. It was great having Mikey in my life because he felt like another son to me as well. He even called me "Ma."

When I heard the news about Mikey, I chose not to tell Nicky. I thought it best to protect my son because I knew he was in a fight for his own life. I didn't want anything that sad to interfere. Instead, I checked in on Mikey without mentioning it to my son. Nicky wouldn't find that unusual.

While there were times that they were in the hospital together and had the comfort of one another, there were also plenty of times that they were in on their own terms.

∞

NICKY'S SURGERY TO remove some of the tumors from his spine was scheduled. Nicky was determined to walk again, and that is why he had so readily agreed to surgery. If it had not been for that drive to walk, I'm not sure if he would've been so agreeable.

After the surgery was over, and he was in recovery, I waited patiently. Sitting outside his room next to the door, Dr. Rausen walked toward me. I knew the look on his face was sadness for us. He told us the tumors were so embedded in areas close to nerves he did not want to further complicate things. He suggested physical therapy. I knew the daily visits from a PT would be a psychological way to keep up the fight.

Later that afternoon, Nicky woke up asking questions.

"Ma, what's going on? Will I ever be able to walk again?" I was lying on the other side of the curtain, awake, staring at the ceiling. In reality, I was begging God to give me the strength to answer my son. With tears rolling down my face, I was choking up, grinding my teeth so hard my body started shaking. I was pretending to be asleep, but Nicky knew I was awake.

"Ma, I know you're not sleeping."

I took a deep breath and softly spoke so I didn't sound like I was having a meltdown.

I smiled when I told him, "No, Nicky, Mommy isn't sleeping. I thought we could take a ride to see Joel Osteen at MSG next week. You love the Garden, right? They gave us front row seats."

On the other side of the curtain, Nicky said, "Sure, I'll go, but I won't be able to walk, right?"

I got up and whipped open the curtain, "Nicky, after MSG, we could go to the Nike store and get the new Jordans. No matter what happens, Nicky, we're never giving up."

I never had it in me to directly respond to my son when he asked these questions. I would twist it so his spirits weren't let down; plus possibly encouraged by an outside source of happiness.

As the weeks passed, the doctors did everything they could, including physical therapy. In the end, while the physical therapy *did* exercise his legs, Nicky had no feeling in the soles of his feet.

∞

AS THANKSGIVING APPROACHED, Nicky was still in the hospital. He held his own, with the exception of not being able to walk. We both agreed he wanted to be home for Thanksgiving. I asked Dr. Rausen if Nicky would be able to come home for the holiday. Without hesitation, he said, "Yes."

As I prepared Thanksgiving dinner, I never expected it would be our last together.

He loved mashed potatoes, the gravy, all the trimmings I made out of love. As I was preparing dinner, his friend Caress came to visit. She and Nicky had a special bond and friendship. I always thought that if Nicky were healthy, they could be that family that Nicky spoke about. She was *perfect* for my son.

That afternoon, as I was carving the turkey, I broke down in tears. I tried hard to keep my mind in the now. But I envisioned past happy holidays with my grandmother, days and years gone by.

During these quiet times, I would talk to her as I did dishes. And beg her to give me the fortitude of grace to show strength for my son.

These moments followed with a big, deep breath as I walked into the living room.

My son was sitting at a tiny table that I had set up for us in the living room. I had gone to back to the kitchen to get the turkey. When I returned, I found Nicky with tears streaming down his face. I was overcome with emotion. My heart ached for him. I wanted to wrap my arms around him and cry right alongside him, but instead, I wrapped my arms around him and held him. I couldn't let him feel my pain because I knew if I did, I would never stop crying.

My mother made his favorite mashed potatoes, and I made sure all of his other favorites were served as well. But Nicky was very weak at this point, and his appetite wasn't the best.

He ate what he could. And I did everything I could do or think of to make sure he was as comfortable as possible.

At the end of the day, Nicky didn't want to leave to go back to the hospital. But they were still doing radiation because the tumors were continuously spreading from his spine to his skull. They did radiation every day now, putting a custom-made net around his head to keep it from moving in that big machine.

Thinking back, the hospital staff was always understanding. That net mask made us all think of Spider-Man. They allowed me to sit close enough to Nicky as his body lifted into the machine, passing my energy to him. I was hoping to remove the cancer from his body and give it all to me.

I wanted Nicky to feel like a man and as if he was in charge of his own destiny, so I began to be more open with him regarding our "behind the scenes" discussions with Dr. Rausen. I made sure he knew that the radiation treatment protocol might not shrink his tumors. We never spoke of death. However, the conversations were not light. I didn't want to have the conversation about death directly with Nicky, so I opted to make him a book out of construction paper. Taking some of my own words and using an excerpt from a book I was reading.

"Nicky, can I share a story with you?"

There was no other way for me to find the courage to discuss it, as I sat vigil by my dying child, except through the words of the woman who nourished my soul, Elisabeth-Kubler Ross.

As I continued, he laid with his head tilted slightly upright, in his forever-peaceful position. His arms gracefully placed in prayer across his chest, staring beyond the ceiling, closing his eyes in between the powerful lines.

Sarcastically, he said, "What if I say no?"

I knew he was adding some humor to the mood, preparing for what might be an intense next half-hour.

My comebacks were usually slightly off the radar.

"Well, Nick, I'll break out the Swiffer for the 10th time today—because I know how much you like your room crispy clean just like your crispy white Ts—while I dance and sing in the room."

In one breath, he said, "No, Ma, that's okay, I'll pass on another Swiffing Broadway musical. Everyone's sleeping. On the other hand, speaking of crispy T-shirts, I do need more before I go home."

"Nicky, I'm on it. I already ordered a couple packages on Amazon yesterday. Plus, I got you some white socks for your new Jordans. It's all good. So, are we ready for your bedtime story?"

"Yes, hurry up. I gotta call Vida before eleven p.m.," Nicky said, with a smile.

"Okay, here we go. All I ask is that you try to remain optimistic. It's only a story, so keep an open mind."

I looked down at the book and then back up quickly.

"I love you, Nicky, with all my heart and soul. This is for us."

This is a story about life and windstorms, about seeds that we plant in the spring, and flowers that bloom in the summer and harvest in the fall.

Death that comes early in life, and to some people late, and what it is all about.

Imagine the very beginning of life and God who created everything—as the sun shines all over the world and warms us. The sun makes the flowers grow and the warm rays that cover the earth—even when clouds make it impossible for us to see them.

God always sees us. His love always shines on us, and it does not matter how small or how big we are, and nothing can ever stop that!

When people are born, they start out as tiny seeds like the dandelion seeds that are blown into the meadow— some end up in the gutter, or a pretty lawn in front of the fairy mansion, some on a flowerbed.

And, so it is with us. We start our life in a rich home or poor family, or an orphanage or beloved by parents who wanted us very much. Like you, Nicky. We wanted you VERY MUCH!

Some people may call it the gamble of life, but you have to remember that God is also in charge of the wind and He cares as much about dandelion seeds as he cares for all living things—especially children— and there are no coincidences in life! He never discriminates, He loves unconditionally, He understands, He does not judge— He is all love.

You and God picked your own parents out of a choice of a billion! You chose them so you can help them to grow and learn, and they can be your teachers, too.

Life is like a school where we are given a chance to learn many things—like to get along with other people, or to understand our feelings, to learn to be honest with ourselves and others, to learn to give and receive love—and when we have passed all the tests—just like in school—we are allowed to graduate—that means we are all allowed to return to our real home—to God where we all came from and where we meet all the people we ever loved—like a family reunion after graduation.

That is the time when we die, when we shed our body, when we have done our work and are able to move on. In the winter, you cannot see life in a tree—but when spring comes, the small green leaves come out—one after another—and in late summer, the tree is full of fruit and has fulfilled its promise—its mission and purpose. In the fall, the leaves fall off—one by one and the tree "goes to rest" over winter.

Some flowers bloom only for a few days—everybody admires and loves them as a sign of spring and hope. Then they die—but they have done what they needed to do! Some flowers bloom for a very long time—people take them for granted, they don't even notice them anymore—the way they treat old people—they watch them sitting in a park until they are gone one day, forever.

Everything in life is a circle; day follows night, spring comes after winter. When a boat disappears behind the horizon, it is not "gone," just out of our sight—God watches over everything that he created—the earth, the sun, trees, flowers and people—who have to get

*through the school of life before they graduate. When
we have done all the work we were sent to earth to do,
we are allowed to shed our body—which imprisons our
soul like a cocoon encloses the future butterfly—and
when the time is right we can let go of it and we will
be free of pain, free of fears and worries—free as a very
beautiful butterfly, returning home to God, which is a
place where we are never alone—where we continue to
grow and to sing and dance, where we are with those
we loved and where we are surrounded by more love
than you can ever imagine!*

When I looked up from reading this passage, Nicky's eyes were
closed. I thought he was sleeping. I got up from my chair and leaned
over to kiss his forehead, and then his arms reached around me.

"Ma, I love you so much. Please don't leave me."

My heart sank, pushing my shoulder against his ear so he
couldn't hear me clenching my teeth, breathing hard through my
nostrils.

"No, Nicky, that'll never happen. I'm here forever and ever.
You could never get rid of me. After all, where will you find such
entertainment?"

I released my hands into the air, bringing that happy mood back
onto the scene. That's what it was all about: a balance of emotions—
how to do it, when to do it, and where to do it never mattered.

Days like that turned into special moments where neither of us
knew what to expect.

In late November, just after Thanksgiving, I stuck my head
out of Nicky's room on 9 East. I'd noticed a lot of activity in front
of Mikey's room. I went back inside and looked out onto the East
River, wondering whether Mikey might need some healing energy.
Something pulled me to go to his room.

I stood at the foot of Mikey's bed. In my peripheral view, I could
see his adopted mother and sister holding each other. I looked at

Mikey, struggling ferociously, with his head going back and forth, grunting as if he wanted to tell me something. But instinctively, I already knew what was about to happen.

I was about to use my special gift on Mikey, as I had in the past with my grandmother when she crossed over.

I took a long breath and exhaled deeply, as I grabbed Mikey's feet with both hands. I stared into his eyes, sending him healing energy. Staring nonstop into his. Within minutes, Mikey stopped shaking his head back and forth, and slowly, the grunting dissipated.

Once I got him to this point of calm, I then telepathically spoke to him: "Mikey, sweetheart, you'll be okay. You've fought long and hard for this moment of peace. We all love you, Mikey. Go home."

At this moment, he stopped, and in my peripheral view, to the left on the ceiling, I saw not one, not two, but three beautifully angelic beings making their way toward Mikey. My eyes made their way back to Mikey. I saw tears flowing, and his eyes gently closing. I took a deep breath again and said, "Mikey, I love you, sweetheart. We'll all see you soon."

I turned around and nodded at Mikey's mom and sister and then I left the room.

As I walked back to Nicky, I felt exhausted. I'd gained some composure and walked into his room with a huge smile. "Honey, I'm back!" I said, as though nothing had happened.

Nicky asked, "Where were you?"

I said, "I went to see what's going on around the unit."

He said, "You're lying, Ma. Where'd you go? Did you go see Mikey?"

I laughed, shaking my head and smiling. "Nicky, nothing gets past you. How can I ever keep a secret from you?"

He said, "You can't. I know everything that's going on."

"I'm sure you do, Nicky. Now, what can we order for dinner?" I said, desperately trying to change the subject.

Changing subjects always helped me to handle the objectives at hand. In this case, I couldn't come right out and tell Nicky about

Mikey. It would crush him, maybe even make him give up on his own fight.

Later that night, he received a text from Pablo while he was sleeping. Pablo was another hospital friend Nicky had met at the beginning of his treatment, who also had Ewing's. Pablo always stayed in touch after his treatment ended while living in Florida. I was sleeping on the cot next to Nicky and heard him crying. *Now, what do I say?* I'd lied to him to buy time. I reached for his hand under the covers from my cot and said, "Nicky, sweetheart, Mommy is so very sorry. I just couldn't find it in my heart to tell you. Please forgive me."

I got up, and he was staring at the ceiling.

I crawled into his bed and held Nicky until morning.

Later that week, I noticed his reading skills were failing, though I thought of it as *not so functional*. Nicky kept asking me for help reading cards and texts. His tumors had become so big that they started to block his hearing and vision. Everything started shutting down.

"Have you discussed with your son whether he wants to stay in the hospital or go home?" Dr. Rausen asked one Sunday afternoon. The question was daunting.

It was inevitable that our fight was about to end.

I asked him, "What do you mean? Stay here or go home?" Tears flowed down my face as Dr. Rausen explained there was nothing more they could do. I needed to make an adult decision for both of us.

I had to think of how to broach this subject with Nicky. *What words would I use?* My heart was pounding. I still wanted to protect my son from any type of emotional pain.

I had to have the courage to ask. So, I just said it.

"Nicky, if you don't want radiation anymore, you don't need it. It's up to you."

His arms were crossed over his chest as he stared up at the ceiling. I sensed he had already spiritually prepared for what may come. As I kissed his forehead, I said, "If you want to come home, you can."

Nicky said, "I want to be in my own bed, Ma. I want to go home."

So, I said, "Okay, we're going home. Today."

Dr. Rausen explained that hospice would come to my house. He made it very clear that he would no longer be able to take my son for any further treatments.

I didn't want to take my son home and make him feel like he was there to die. I still wanted him to have hope. I begged Dr. Rausen not to end the treatments. He told me not to worry. He would make sure Nicky would still be able to receive some care at the clinic, even though he knew it wasn't necessary.

Dr. Rausen ordered the hospice nurses to come in each morning to draw blood. If they felt he needed a transfusion of platelets, then we would call an ambulette to take him for the transfusion. This is how it went for the last three weeks. I will be forever grateful to Dr. Rausen. Because of him and the continued treatments, Nicky was encouraged to keep going and never to give up hope.

However, Nicky just wanted to be home.

I remember one time, Nicky saw butterflies in his bedroom.

He called me in there one evening, and, in a low whispered tone, he said, "Ma, look at all those beautiful butterflies in the corner up there."

I looked, and my eyes popped open. "Oh, my gosh, Nicky. Look at them! They're so beautiful, sweetheart."

A week later, I was sleeping on the couch, and he was banging on the wall with his cane.

"Ma, Ma! Hurry up! Come here."

I peeked around the door. "Nicky, are you okay?"

"Ma, go to the back door. There's a man there. Tell him to go away," he demanded, firmly.

And so I did. I felt frightened.

"Okay, Nicky, here I go babe," I said, as I opened the door.

"Hello, hello? Please go away. My son doesn't want to talk to you! How was that, Nicky?" I asked him.

"Good, Ma. Now we can go to sleep," he replied, assuring me.

I laid back down but couldn't fall asleep. What is going on? I wondered to myself. Is he seeing what I think he is seeing? Is he controlling his destiny?

All I knew was that Nicky was *now* in charge.

∞

WE WENT TO the hospital by ambulance every day and came home in the same way.

There was always someone willing to put a smile on Nicky's face. A faithful friend from the community adored Nicky, and he was instrumental in every area when it came to doing something. In the middle of December, former major league Yankees pitcher David Cone visited Nicky. My son, a Yankees fan, was thrilled. Cone brought him a signed glove and baseball, and he also signed Nicky's hat.

Just like Thanksgiving, Nicky's wish was to be home for Christmas, and hospice care allowed him to do that.

I held a huge Christmas party for him on December 20, the day of one of his blood transfusions. About thirty of us decorated our tiny apartment in Tuckahoe. We spent the entire day cooking and preparing the house for his welcome home—it was a transfusion day, back in Manhattan—we all waited patiently inside the house.

At seven p.m., the ambulance brought Nicky home on the stretcher. He was taken into my bedroom to get ready. His sister came into his room, as a surprise. When he saw Bianca, tears streamed down his face, and he could barely speak.

His buddy, John, got him cleaned up and gave him a shave. His friends were all talking outside the bedroom door. Nicky started to become nervous and asked them to wait outside and come in after he was seated in his wheelchair in the corner of the living room.

I peeked into the bedroom and asked, "Nicky, do you like Mommy's hair down or up in a bun?"

He said, "Leave it down, Ma. You look beautiful. Don't ever cut your hair."

The music was playing, and all the kids were outside waiting to come in. It was a cold December evening. I opened the door, and each one walked right up to Nicky, giving him a high-five, a kiss, or a hug, and they all surrounded him.

It was like a scene from *The Godfather*. His friends offered to get him a plate explaining they'd made his favorite dishes, such as Penne Alla Vodka, Baked Ziti, and bread from Arthur Avenue.

The evening was going smoothly, talking about his new sneakers and sweatsuit and other things. Then, all of a sudden, Nicky started crying. I walked over to him, holding his cheeks.

"What's wrong, sweetheart?"

"I want everyone to leave." His tears were flowing. "This song reminds me of Mikey. I want to be left alone."

At that moment, I quietly asked his friends to go. I told them he wasn't feeling well. Soon after, I cuddled Nicky in his bed until morning.

∞

I WAS ENCOURAGED to request Father Anthony to come in each day in the early morning after his 8:30 a.m. mass to give Nicky communion and pray with us.

A few days before Nicky transitioned, Father Anthony stood over us, as we laid in his bed, with his arms raised and said, "Nicky, you remind me of Jesus. You will be welcomed into Heaven's gates with open arms." I saw Nicky's eyes well up, and I squeezed his hand.

Father Anthony came by early in the morning on December 26 to give Nicky communion, and also, his last rites. Every night, I slept next to my son on an air mattress on the floor. But, that night, when all the lights were out, my son asked me to crawl into bed with him.

At that point, Nicky was very frail. The high doses of chemo and steroids had caused him to gain weight. His face was round and yellow, and his brown hair was scattered over his scalp in patches. He had lost most of his sight, and his speech had slowed.

He had also lost all feeling from his hips to his legs because of the tumors that continuously grew.

So, that night seemed to be a special one. We talked, laughed, took pictures with his camera, and cuddled. I wrapped myself around him and didn't him go until we woke up the next morning. I told Nicky we would be going on a lot of trips after the New Year.

He told me, "Mom, next year is going to be a better year for you."

When he did not include himself in that sentence, I knew what he was saying.

On the morning of December 27, I did what I did every morning. I gave Nicky a warm bath from head to toe. His skin was so dry, so I reached for his favorite cucumber moisturizer and slowly rubbed the lotion into his skin.

∞

ONE DAY, TOWARD the end, Nicky was taken to the hospital for another blood transfusion. He still had high hopes that he would beat his cancer and he was willing to do anything to fight it.

I secretly prayed for a miracle. *God, I'm here, Michele Cynthia Bell,* I begged, *give my life to Nicolas Anthony, my son.* Maybe, just maybe, this time would be different.

We were transported from home by ambulance for a blood transfusion at Hassenfeld. At six p.m., we left the doctor's office, and shortly, we were stuck in the middle of New York City traffic on 31st Street and the FDR. While we were stuck just underneath the entrance to the FDR, Nicky stopped breathing.

The ambulance immediately took us back to the hospital, and we were admitted to the ER. I freaked out and time stood still! Yet it was also moving fast, and I felt as though we were running out of it.

I heard Nicky saying, from the other side of the curtain, from underneath his oxygen mask, "Mom, calm down, it's going to be okay."

When we left the hospital that evening, we were sent home with only two small tanks of oxygen. They were so small that they would provide only fifty minutes of oxygen—just enough that, if my son needed to be rushed back to the hospital, he would have enough until we could get another one from the pharmacy.

After we arrived home, and Nicky was settled in his bed, the paramedics told me they needed to take the oxygen tanks back with them.

With the paramedics gone. I guess I began freaking out a bit. I went to Nicky's room to let him know we needed to head back to the hospital right away because there would be no oxygen in the house until the morning when the pharmacy would bring a tank.

Nicky didn't want to leave. Reassuring me, he gently stated, "Mom, I'm going to be okay."

I left his room not knowing whether to call the paramedics back or not. A close family friend was there, who thankfully took charge and called 911. Within minutes, another ambulance was sitting in our driveway.

I felt exhausted and drained. Each and every night, I slept in the same room as Nicky, and I woke up as many as ten to fifteen times a night to make sure he was still breathing.

For the third time in one day, we arrived at Lawrence Hospital. They told us that the next morning we would have an oxygen tank at the house, and Nicky would be able to go home in the afternoon. We were both extremely relieved.

Nicky loved being home, back in his own bed. By now, he was so exhausted, it didn't take him long to fall asleep. I then did what I did every night: I stood guard. Ready to react in a second's notice to anything that posed danger.

The following day—it was now December 29—after we returned home from the hospital in the afternoon, I gave Nicky some morphine, as prescribed by Dr. Rausen, because he was in so much pain. The tumors continued to grow, and the ones in his head had grown to the point where Nicky could no longer hear me.

Not long after I had given him the morphine, Nicky fell asleep once again. He couldn't stay awake no matter how hard he tried. In many ways, this was a blessing for him. At least, in his sleep, I knew he didn't feel any pain. But regardless of his loss of hearing, I had made a tape of soothing music he could listen to with headphones. It was the same music I had listened to while in labor with him.

A couple of mothers of Nicky's friends stopped by to offer me support. I truly appreciated it, but deep down, I didn't want them there. I knew I had precious and borrowed time left with my son. Finally, I simply asked them to leave.

They were very gracious and understood my request, and I was truly thankful for that.

It was now around seven-thirty p.m. on Dec. 29. Hospice came over and directed us to give him morphine to alleviate his pain and help him end his fight for life.

I sang "You and Me Against the World" to Nicky. I spoke to him in his ear. He was so peaceful, he would look at me and smile.

At about eight-fifteen p.m., I was finally alone in the room with my son. I raised my hands and said, "Please God, I release my son. Take this pain away from him."

But he wasn't releasing. One of the hospice nurses told me that Nicky couldn't let go until he knew I was going to be okay.

She said, "Tell him you're going to be okay so that he won't worry about you."

I whispered in his ear, "Nicky, Mommy loves you so much. And I'm going to miss you like no other. You're a gift to me, and I am going to be okay. Please don't worry about Mommy. I'll be strong for you."

I raised my hands to God and thanked Him aloud for blessing me with such a wonderful son. And I asked Him, "Please take my son in your loving arms and free him from his pain."

I then kissed Nicky and said in his ear, "Nicky, please watch over Mommy. I love you, my baby."

As I pulled away, his eyes opened and looked right at me, very intently.

He said from under his oxygen mask, "Mom, I love you. I'm going home."

I felt like I had been punched in the gut. It felt as though his soul passed through me on his journey to the other side. I collapsed and passed out on the hardwood floor just below the edge of his bed. Someone must have heard the fall, picked me up, walked me outside onto the front porch, and wrapped me in a blanket.

My body was numb and stiff sitting in the chair on the porch. I could barely move. Ironically, these were the very moments Nicky was crossing over. His body, too, was becoming numb and stiff. I could feel it.

Within seconds, loud sounds came from the other side of the window.

Suddenly, the porch door swung open, and the hospice nurse, in a somber tone, told me, "Nicky's just passed."

I jumped up from the chair, ran into the house, tripped over the couch, finally, and stood at the foot of his bed.

For a moment, I felt an out-of-body experience. Although I was surrounded by family and friends, I felt like I was in the room with strangers. Lights were on, and the oxygen mask was off Nicky's face. I started screaming for them to put the mask back on and for everyone to leave. They tried to calm me down, but I couldn't stop crying and screaming.

Within a few minutes, everyone left the room to leave me alone with my son.

He looked so peaceful. His hands were crossed on his stomach, and his eyes were closed forever. I rubbed lotion into his feet, which were very chapped, and on his legs. I felt like giving him a bath. I didn't know what else to do. So, I lay down next to him and held him tightly.

SEVENTEEN

SAYING GOODBYE

N EWS TRAVELS QUICKLY. In what seemed like a very short time after his passing, suddenly hundreds of Nicky's friends were lined up outside our home with candles and flowers. The line stretching the entire length of the block. I invited them in to say goodbye to their best friend. I couldn't believe how many kids came by. There was so much pain in their eyes. I'm grateful that my son had been blessed with so many beautiful friends.

I strongly felt I must do justice to him in his passing. In the weeks leading up to his funeral and while in solitude, I had begun collecting my thoughts to write down the sentiments I needed to say to family and friends, as Nicky slept. I limited visits to close friends, family, and nurses. I spent sleepless nights writing and trying to prepare his eulogy.

My thoughts felt scrambled, but I managed to write what I thought would be an honor to Nicky... something that would preserve his memory. With tears flowing down my face, I thanked God for the beautiful blessing He had given me eighteen years earlier.

I also tried to understand why He had taken my child from my heart. But was Nicky *taken* from me? I believe that, when God puts love and compassion in our hearts, He is offering us the opportunity to make a difference in a person's life. Nicky made a huge difference in my life. You can't take what someone's experienced in their life from them. His voice echoed back from his birthday party, "You have given me the meaning of life, and that I had no right to expect. That no one can ever take away from me." Through Nicky's strength in facing challenges with confidence, through his true contentment, born of simple things, I felt proud to call him my son. So, with that in mind, I was determined to honor his life at his funeral.

∞

WE HELD NICKY'S spectacular funeral in Eastchester. The day before we laid him out was absolutely heart-wrenching. I went with my mother to the funeral home to pick out Nicky's casket. I selected a black one with silver handles, fully open and lined with white satin. I knew he would look handsome in the pinstriped suit with red shirt and tie, the same one he had worn on his birthday.

They had prepped him downstairs and asked if I wanted to view him, but I refused. If I did, I knew it would be too difficult to leave him.

The flowers started to come in from all over. The community support was overwhelming—there were so many cards, so many flowers, and so many people lined up outside before Nicky's wake began. Shortly before they all came, I got my own time alone with Nicky.

There he was in his casket, quietly laid out, surrounded by beautiful flowers with a bed of red roses.

I couldn't believe how handsome and peaceful he looked. I moved around in shock, knowing with each moment, I was a step closer to never seeing Nicky's physical being again.

At the casket, I leaned in and hugged him tightly, not wanting to let go. I pulled away and fixed his hair and brushed one of my tears off his face. Holding his hands that wrapped around his rosary beads, I fiddled with his tie and shoes to make sure his feet lay straight. He looked flawless.

I took a deep breath and walked back into the silent hallway where I could see his loving friends waiting. As I walked back into that room where we had arranged a personal memorial montage, I told myself, "He's just sleeping." But I knew better. The beautiful face that had always tried to hide the pain was now very peaceful.

Once again the lyrics played in my head to the song we sang together during our drives to NYC....then remembering our memories alone will get us through. Think about the days of me and you. You and me against the world.

In the other room, his birthday photomontage was playing, with his CD-mix music in the background. Around us were posters of photos and all the memories of his life. The DJ at Nicky's birthday had made up a special CD. Everyone could sit and be closest to Nicky in this room.

I peeked out the window, and I couldn't believe the swarms of people who were standing in line to see my son during these cold December days.

The line went up the hill almost three blocks. Police cars blocked off the streets because of the number of people who came to his two-day wake. It all felt overwhelming. My only saving grace was that I didn't leave his side. I stood and greeted everyone.

I am forever grateful for the respect they showed by coming to say goodbye to my son. I watched people gaze at Nicky with so much love. Some people drove for hours to be there—my mother's friends from church and Nicky's father's family from upstate.

∞

MOURNERS PLACED NOTES and precious mementos inside Nicky's casket. His sendoff was much less a goodbye, and more like a celebration of his life. His friends created a memorial brochure, which we handed out to everyone, with Nicky's photo on the cover.

On the day of the funeral, I placed special memories of our life together into the casket, along with a letter. I prayed to Nicky to give me the strength to keep my composure as I stared at everyone. It seemed like lips talking to me, movement without a voice. Holding back tears, I stood there, totally numb.

Father Anthony, the priest who gave Nicky communion each day while he was in hospice at home, prepared the most loving speech imaginable. He spoke of meeting Nicky for the first time, how my son put out his hand for a handshake and thanked him for coming.

He spoke of Nicky's great faith in God, of the special love between a mother and her son that he witnessed. He also spoke about the last time he saw Nicky, just two days before he transitioned.

He would arrive early in the morning to pray with us in bed and give Nicky communion, and as sick as Nicky was, he never said, "No." And Nicky always told him, "Thank you, Father," in spite of his struggle to speak.

Father Anthony made the sign of the cross as he spoke, in days leading up to that last time. And said, "Nicky, you remind me of Jesus. Your strength and sacrifice are how Jesus walked his path. You are a blessing to all who know you. You will enter the house of many mansions. 'In my Father's house there are many mansions: if it were not so, I would have told you. I go to prepare a place for you.'"

Then I read my son's eulogy, which I had written a month and a half before he transitioned.

∞

"Today is the most difficult day in my family's life, as we gather to say farewell to our son, grandson, brother, and loyal friend. What a glorious day that we are all here together, and you are my son's for the day. I'm

going to break precedent to tell you my one wish— that you all would experience a life as lucky as mine, where you could wake up one morning and say, 'I don't want or need anything more.' Eighteen years went by in the blink of an eye. I loved Nicky from the moment he was born and every minute in between.

As I express intimate moments of the bountiful unconditional love we shared between mother and son, know in your hearts of the unconditional love Nicky had for all of you.

As I looked into his eyes on June 20, 1987, I knew my life's mission was to be sure that Nicky made his beautiful journey through time with unconditional love and happiness, and that he knew what real love truly is. Nicky has shown me the meaning of life, which I had no right to expect and no one will ever take that from me.

Those of you here and elsewhere, who sincerely knew Nick, are already aware of the type of person he was. The words you will hear from me are already in your memory. To those who are not as fortunate, these words will give you a sense of the type of man he was and an ideal to strive for.

My son has often been described as a gentle soul. He was pure at heart and had great compassion for the world around him. He had a way with people. He made them feel comfortable, and they gravitated toward him. Nicky exuded kindness and drew generosity and altruism from everyone he touched. He was everyone's best friend. To say Nick was polite is an understatement. Since his early years, he showed vast respect and concern for everyone around him. Even throughout the past four and a half years of tormenting hospital stays and chemotherapy treatments, he never once failed to thank his doctors, nurses, transport workers, or anyone else, whether they gave him a meal, assisted him or performed another painful procedure.

Nicky never lost his kindhearted attitude. Up until his last breath, he never doubted his faith or the plan that God had for him. His last words he whispered in my ear were, "Mom, I love you, I'm going home." At that moment, I pulled back slowly as tears rolled down my cheeks. I looked at him, his eyes opening slowly for that one last glance into each other's eyes. As his eyes closed, I felt as though a basketball had come through my stomach. I had a mesmerizing experience of rebirth as I held my stomach and collapsed to the floor on the side of his bed. My body was completely drained. The energy between us during those moments powerfully took over every cell inside. I now carry his soul inside of me for the rest of my life.

Nicky was the quiet baby, while his sister bubbled with energy. He was the little guy who loved to share stories before he went to sleep or play a joke on you while you were asleep. He was a polite young man who simply enjoyed everything life offered. He grew into a man with a beautiful mind and an even more beautiful soul. He had a great offbeat sense of humor that caressed his friends and family, and anyone around him. Nicky also cherished his time alone.

He loved listening to music, playing his Xbox or just quietly praying in his room. My son and I enjoyed taking vacations together and walking on one of our favorite beaches in the Caribbean. He was the son who would watch my tearjerker girly films with me and play little jokes on me; the son who loved to go out to great restaurants a few times a week after chemo, simply because we both loved to spend quality time together talking about life and our future. He shared my love for life. We were a team and very much in sync with each other. Whenever I needed his input or reassurance, he offered me words of guidance.

I can still see the boy who came into our lives, with a smile always on his face. Nicky had the ability to light up a room with his magnificent aura. He was the perfect son. I often told Nick that he was my hero and that I was forever blessed that God had allowed me to be his mother and source of guidance. Yet, I felt he was my guidance. My angel, my best friend, he lived his life in a way that epitomized strength and understanding, never seeking pity from anyone. He kept giving it his all when anyone else would have quit long ago. He never complained.

Hero is an overused word, but in Nick's case, it was an understatement. He was a man of true and honest kindness. Nicky loved his friends like they were his brothers and sisters. Before, during and after his illness, they were and will continue to be his brothers and sisters, never leaving his side for a moment. They would sit and talk and laugh and reminisce about the good times in the hospital until the wee hours of the morning. They stood by his side and made him feel like he was one of their own. They never excluded him and made him feel very special. He loved each and every one of you. I thank you for being there for my Nick.

One last person I feel the need to mention is Dr. Aaron Rausen. He was such an important man in my son's life because he gave us extra time together. I think he knew how Nicky felt about him. When Dr. Rausen allowed him to go home for the last time, Nicky said, "Thank you, Dr. Rausen, you were like a father to me. Thank you for everything." He always treated my son like a man, with love and respect. He gave him the dignity that he so justly deserved …

A Rare Blend of Medical Mystery and Human Compassion

Nicky will live on in me and in all of you."

As I looked up, I saw Dr. Rausen at the back of the room. He'd traveled all the way up by train from Manhattan. Showing in his presence how much genuine, high regard this man of medicine had for Nick. My son had that much of an impact on him.

After my eulogy, Dr. Rausen spoke as did so many of Nicky's friends. We all took time at our good-byes.

In 2001, at the beginning of fall, Dr. Rausen had set in motion the treatment for Nicky. I was in mortal fear and shock, and coming under Dr. Rausen's care was the best thing that could have happened. I immediately knew that he was brilliant and that he had phenomenal inner strength and resolve. He was direct and real with us, and supremely knowledgeable about every aspect of Nick's care.

He was kind to us, and he had authority and humanity we trusted. Dr. Aaron Rausen was the "Superman" for each child he treated. His wisdom and compassion had no fears to fight against the most devastating fear: a child with cancer. I am terribly sad, yet relieved Nicky's pain-free.

∞

A FEW MONTHS after Nicky had transitioned, I stopped by Dr. Rausen's office. As I walked in, I noticed a cane leaning up against his desk. I never uttered a word of the thoughts that were going through my head. I intuitively knew he had cancer. My empath abilities can be a curse at times, sadly knowing beforehand what is happening.

He stood up with the help of his cane and shook my hand.

Gracefully, he held out his hand, and said, "Sit down, Miss Bell."

I smiled and stared beyond his horn-rimmed glasses.

"Thank you, from the bottom of my heart, for taking Nicky under your wing in so many ways. I'm beyond grateful for all you did these last four and half years."

With his hands crossed on his desk, his head perched up looking at me he said, "Miss Bell, you're one of the most unique mothers I've *ever* met. I admire you greatly for the care and compassion you bestowed upon Nicolas." (He always called him Nicolas.) "He was very lucky to have a mother like you. You went above your call of duty as a mother. He loved you very much."

This was our last conversation together. Within a year, Dr. Rausen had passed away on the very floor he spent his entire career as a Professor and Oncologist at the NYU hospital with his children and medical staff.

There were many people concerned about Nicky—the nurses, the hospital staff, and friends—but only a few can be mentioned today. You know who you are.

Your selfless acts will never be forgotten.

The many friends who would send cards daily, offer meals at local restaurants after the long days at the hospital, holy water from Lourdes, the endless outpouring of support from the community— we thank you all.

Nicky is my special angel, but to be able to share him with all of you has been my pleasure. He was and is our special gift from God who will never be forgotten.

∞

FATHER ANTHONY'S WORDS at Nicky's mass were unspeakably intense. As he spoke about us, I got up from the pew and wrapped my arms around Nicky's casket, burning inside, knowing I would never be able to hold him again.

It was a cold and dark day. I tried to walk steadily next to his casket, hiding my fear and deep sadness under my hat. I kept praying to Nicky to give me the strength to keep calm. As we got into the car, the line of cars waiting behind ours stretched for three blocks.

The town police escorted us through Eastchester, Tuckahoe, and Scarsdale. We passed the home where he grew up, the basketball court where he played every day, and the schools he attended. Then we drove on the Bronx River Parkway to Ferncliff Cemetery in Hartsdale, where my son's remains were to be cremated.

On the way there, I stared out the window. If people spoke to me, I failed to listen. I just wanted to be left alone. I remember I had asked God to help me get through the final moments of saying goodbye to my best friend and son.

We all joined together in the small chapel. Nicky's casket was placed in the front, behind a gate of some sort. I couldn't hear anyone talking to me. His casket was slid onto a cart—that movement reminded me of all the times he had been rolled into surgery when he would wave to me and throw me a kiss. But this time, he would be waving and throwing me a kiss from above. The knowledge of what was going to happen after a short prayer was killing me inside.

But I knew Nicky would be in a Pieta (an urn), and I knew he would be next to me for the rest of my life. And, ultimately, we would reunite in the end.

∞

I COULDN'T EVEN catch my breath. I felt numb sitting there in that small chapel. I wondered what everyone would think if I got up and stopped the entire ceremony and asked to see him just one last time. But then my son spoke to my heart and told me, "Mom, stay calm. I'm with you always."

I bowed my head, watching my tears fall onto the cold marble floor.

I could barely walk that frigid afternoon—leaving the funeral home and chapel—without the help of the funeral directors holding and escorting me to each location. I felt my knees shaking as I tried to keep my composure. Without the compassion of the funeral directors, I would have more than likely fallen to the ground.

Walking out of the chapel, I gazed at the sky, and I asked myself, *Where is my son.*

His ashes are kept in his urn. His Pieta depicts
a mother's unconditional love

EIGHTEEN

INTO THE LIGHT

I T WAS THEN, at that quiet moment, in honor of my son, that I started to ponder what kind of life Nicky would wish me to have.

My soul knew I could not withstand the grueling emotion I was about to face.

I had thoughts of years gone by…to my grandmother's last days. How ill she was, and how I'd gone upstate to celebrate her, what I called, *arrival back home*.

In early spring 1998, I got on the train leaving Westchester to Albany to say goodbye to the woman who listened when I was sad and taught me how to cook, remembering the loyalty that she professed beneath her breath. She was my rock, and she took no shit when I was bullied as a child by other girls in the neighborhood.

As I approached her room at St. Mary's, I took a deep breath, saying to myself, "I must face the pain." I slowly approached her bedside. I gently grabbed her hand in the hospital room. She was breathing strangely enough for me to quickly start praying. I bowed my head to her hip as I kneeled next to her bedside, squeezing my eyes tight enough not to show tears. I started to talk internally to my grandmother. I knew she could hear me.

"Gram, I adore you so much. I will miss you very, very much because you were not only my grandmother, but you took the time to talk kindly to me and listen to my fears without judgment."

All of a sudden, my body felt like melted butter. I felt like I was levitating into the light. I was in the most beautiful serene place I had ever been. As I admired the beauty of the light, I was drawn closer, feeling the radiant warmth, infinite love, and lasting peace. I felt as if I were home in the light. Before I was further engulfed, I became aware of many spirits. They surrounded, embraced, and supported my journey with the gentleness, knowledge, and guidance.

I looked up, as we were elevating into the light, realizing that a group of spiritual beings was awaiting her on this celestial plane. At this moment, it was my time to return to where I left my grandmother in the hospital. The overwhelming love and happiness of that place was so inviting.

I looked up at my mother and asked her, "Ma, did you feel anything strange?"

She just looked at me. "I have no idea what you're talking about. Let's go grab a bite to eat."

That evening, a few hours later, we got a call from the hospital. My grandmother *had* crossed over, and thankfully, I was blessed to be there to guide her into the unknown.

My experience with my grandmother is something I will never forget.

That was my very first experience connecting with the other side, as Sylvia Brown, a world-renowned medium would say. I prefer the term "going home."

It was the beginning of my true spiritual journey as a Life Path number 11 and learning more about near-death experiences.

These encounters have prepared me to have newfound faith and strength to take care of my son and presently taking on the role as a caregiver for my mother.

Rare occurrences like these have prepared me to face each life obstacle. I understand and embrace them. However, at times, I am so tired.

After I helped my grandmother to cross over, I went to visit Sylvia Brown to validate that what had occurred was real.

She explained, "My dear, you have beautiful gifts that you must learn how to use. You have the ability to heal people. Teach yourself to commune with this special blessing for your next journey."

After our meeting, I immediately went to Barnes & Noble to get all the books related to channeling and psychic teachings.

I spent the next months reading and absorbing all of this knowledge. I did not want to learn how to use these gifts but rather, *understand* that what I had to offer would enhance someone's life. It was all so overwhelming. I wanted to the take baby steps required so I was better able to understand myself.

One evening in December 2000, I was shopping in Lord & Taylor when a young petite girl walked up to me.

She said, "I don't want to frighten you. I'm a medium. Do you know what that is?"

My eyebrows arched and my eyes widened, as I said, "Why, of course. I met Sylvia Brown not long ago."

This petite girl told me she had a message for me. I asked her to come to my house, and I gave her my address and phone, in case she got lost. I quickly walked to my car and drove home at high speed to make sure no one was home before she came inside.

She started walking up the front steps, and I opened the door and said, "I'm so glad you found your way."

What she told me was brief and to the point.

She explained that, as she was driving, she saw a little petite woman with red hair, and she asked what her name was, and the woman told her, "Mary."

Sitting on the couch in silence, I asked, "What did she say to you?"

"She wants me to tell you how proud she is of you for the way you are raising your children."

At that moment, tears welled up in my eyes. I shook my head and told her, "Thank you for this validation. It means the world to me."

She continued to offer vivid advice regarding a current relationship, saying, "Stay away from the limo man. He isn't sincere in your quest for love."

As this young girl was getting ready to leave, she mentioned Nicky and my father by explaining that my father often visits Nicky in his room and stands around Nicky's trophies.

"He's watching over Nicky."

I understood this completely because a Nicky would hop in bed with me during the night, scared at seeing a tall man around his trophies in his room, who he thought was Poppi.

I met several like-minded people as the years went by and the next adventure in my journey was getting closer.

Most souls who go through the heavenly process pass through a tunnel and toward the light of God. They return home to the place they came from on the other side.

Nicky's friend Mikey was another soul I helped cross over into the light. The next day, one of the meal servers asked me if she could pray with Nicky after his lunch.

I said, "Let me ask my son, and I'll look for you."

She was a petite Spanish lady, filled with so much light, and she loved the teenage boys on the ninth floor.

Under the circumstances, I felt this was a message. I gently asked Nicky if it was okay if she came after lunch to pray with him in silence.

Nicky said, "Yes, Mom," with his eyes closed.

Later that afternoon, she returned to pick up the lunch trays, and I sat outside Nicky's door waiting for her.

I said, "Nicky's resting, but he'd welcome your prayer vigil. I'll wait outside here so we don't have any disturbance."

With this in mind, I bowed my head in silence outside the door to pray on my own.

Within five minutes, she opened the door. I stood up, and she held my face, saying, "You're in God's grace. He is with your son."

I closed my eyes and took a breath knowing I had to go back in the room to relieve my son's emotions from whatever had occurred.

Quickly, I put on that happy smile, opened the door and walked over to his bedside. He was lying with his hands folded across his chest. As I looked closer, tears were rolling down the sides of his face.

I grabbed a tissue and gently wiped his cheeks and asked, "Nicky, are you okay? What happened? Please tell Mommy. Take your time and relax, baby. I'm here and never leaving your side."

He said, "I saw Mikey." His face tightened with more tears, as he tried to explain exactly what he'd seen.

Meanwhile, I leaned over to hug him, to feel his sadness so I would be able to absorb any pain.

I whispered in his ear, "I'm here, sweetheart, whenever you're ready to release what transpired. You can share it with Mommy. I understand."

He then opened his eyes and stared at the ceiling.

He said, "I saw Mikey…" I waited for more. It took a long time, but I waited between Nicky's breaths.

Then he could say more… "He was in a long tunnel, and I saw a white light…" still more seconds passed. We had the time, this was Mikey's last time with Nicky. "From far away, he looked like Mikey. He had all his hair."

"Oh my God, Nicky, that is so beautiful…"

"…and he didn't look sick anymore…"

I listened as he explained to me what I have been learning about with my experiences. I knew Nicky was ready to make his own journey into the light soon. With this in mind, that was when I ran across the street to the bookstore and scoured the grief section for books that could help me, and eventually, help Nicky through this process.

I kept grabbing the *Elisabeth Kubler-Ross* books. I knew I would be able to pass these tender words onto Nicky when needed.

Enough years have passed since Nicky has gone home. My understanding of the afterlife is now more pronounced than ever.

On a recent retreat with some friends, I was in the backseat en route to our destination up to Bear Mountain in Westchester, NY.

Without full knowledge of my son, one of the girls turned to me and said, "Michele, there's a man looking out for you. He's your warrior on the other side. At one time, you were both together in another life. You were his teacher, and in this life, he's your teacher."

Once again, a profound validation had come through.

From time to time, I experience these little bursts of acknowledgments all in Divine timing. I'll repeat it again, Everything happens for a reason. You trust, pray, and trust again that the higher power in which you believe is truly watching over you.

On June 20, 2016, I drove down to Brooklyn to visit a friend who is a celebrity tattoo artist. I'd seen a particular symbol throughout the years and was waiting for Divine timing to get a tattoo of it. The Unalome tattoo was placed inside my inner lower right arm. That evening, I drove up to the Berkshires, in Stockbridge, Massachusetts. It wa the night of the solstice full moon.

After returning and sitting outside for a while on the lawn, I went inside. As I sat down, a young girl walked past me. I turned around and watched her push the elevator button. My heart was beating hard as I looked at her back which was tattooed, covered in two huge angel wings. I had no time to decide whether or not to approach her. I just hopped off the bench and ran over.

This was definitely Divine intervention. I said to her, "Hi, I'm so sorry to stop you, but I must share this with you." She stared at me as I babbled. "Look at my tattoo! It's wrapped in plastic because I just got it hours ago in honor of my son. It's his birthday today, and he would have been 29."

I showed her the little path explaining the swirls of confusion twisting path to a single line reaching enlightenment. "It's an Unalome, which means a journey to enlightenment."

She was taken back by my explanation.

"Your angel wings gravitated me to come over. His non-profit was called Skipper's Angel Wings. And he wanted the same tattoo before he passed away. He was unable to do so because of his platelets. Always too low. So I just wanted to share the story with you and thank you for this sign." I looked down at her badge. It was turned around, and I couldn't see her name. "What's your name?" I asked. She turned her badge around. Her name was Nicky. I was so moved by this sign that I posted it all over my social media accounts.

It sounds like I might be jumping around from time to time, but I have to also to tell you of this one moment. The night that Nicky crossed over, I took photos of his empty bed capturing his childhood, with Ernie his teddy bear on the pillow. That evening, I slept in his bed with his Nextel phone. It rang at four a.m. It was an unknown number, and when I answered it in my sleep, there was silence on the other end.

The following morning, his phone rang again. My mother asked, "Where's that ringing coming from?" I was baffled, as it was under my pillow the entire night. All of sudden, she found his flip-phone in Nicky's slippers that she wore that night to bed. *In the kitchen.*

Just before his wake, the following day, I went to CVS to pick up the photos of his bedroom I took the evening that he passed. As I looked, I saw three orbs just above the stuffed animals. I knew it was Nicky, my grandmother, and my father. I felt comforted that Nicky was with me. I got into the car and turned on the radio. One of his favorite songs was playing, "Alright," by Red Carpet.

As the days, weeks, and months passed, I was anxious to talk to Nicky. I went on eBay to find an Ouiji board. Of course, in my desperation, I wanted to bring him forth. As I was preparing to do so one night, my hairdresser came over to color my hair. I asked her if she would help me communicate with my son.

I blessed the house with sage and lit white candles all around the living room. My list of questions was short. All I wanted was to communicate with Nicky.

We sat down on the living room floor staring at one another, and

I asked my first question, "Nicky, I am so lost without you… what do I do with my life?" After seven minutes, the planchette started moving to the letters W-O-R-K.

I lifted up my hands from the board, asking my hairdresser if she'd moved it, and she said, "No."

I knew this was Nicky coming through because I felt no evil around us. I began crying hysterically, and she encouraged me to continue asking questions. I asked Nicky, "Are you with anyone?" The planchette moved and spelled out M-I-K-E-Y, his friend who had passed a month earlier. At that moment, I knew she was not forcing the movement because Stephie had no clue who Mikey was.

That evening after she left, my mind raced as I thought how powerful Nicky's spirit is on the other side.

Angel Wings tattoo

Meeting a new friend, Nicky on Solstice Moon-June
20th-Nicky's 29th Birthday in the Berkshires

ANGELS BY MY SIDE

IF SOMETHING WERE TO HAPPEN TO ME, IF GOD WERE
TO TAKE ME AWAY FROM THIS EARTH.
HE WOULD BRING ME TO A BETTER PLACE. ONE THAT
I DESERVE.

LIFE HAS BEEN TOUGH AT TIMES, AND THERE'S PAIN
THAT I HAVE KNOWN.
BUT MY FEAR OF DEATH HAS LESSONED, THROUGH
THIS I HAVE GROWN.

I'VE SAT LONELY AND SAD, AND MANY TEARS I HAVE
CRIED.
BUT I WAS NEVER ALONE,
THERE WERE ANGELS BY MY SIDE.

I HAVE PAID MANY DUES FOR MISTAKES I HAVE MADE,
SO I KNOW IT WOULD BE ALRIGHT IF GOD TOOK ME
AWAY.

UP TO HEAVEN I WOULD GO, WITH ANGELS I WOULD
PLAY,
WITH BEAUTIFUL CONTENTMENT, AND I WOULD
NEVER BE AFRAID.

IF GOD HAD A SCORE CHART. I TRUELY BELIEVE;
FOR NOW HE'D HAVE PICKED OUT SOMETHING
WONDERFUL FOR ME.

Michele Bell

I WILL PATIENTLY WAIT WITH ANGELS BY MY SIDE.
AS GOD WILL GUIDE ME, WITH HIS PURPOSE I WILL
ABIDE.

CHARLES NICOLAS BELL (NICKY'S GRANDFATHER-LIFE
PATH 11)
ARTIST, POET, WRITER
1994

Artwork made with love by Danielle Repetti

Excerpts taken from interview after the Red Devil treatments

The scars of Bell's ordeal during this recent phase of recovery are more physical than emotional, thanks to his positive attitude and "help from my family and friends." He even jokes with people who notice the foot-long scar on his leg where the tumor was removed and the roundish mark on his chest where the chemotherapy portal was inserted.

"I tell kids the scar on my leg is from a shark attack and the one on my chest is a bullet wound," Bell laughed. "You know, they believe it until tell him the real story."

"I'd like to write a book maybe," Bell said. "I'd like to tell people about what it was to go through it. It might help some other kid who has to face it. I might also want to become a psychologist, to get to know how people think and to help them."

For now, Nicholas, who is not allowed to participate in contact or physically demanding sports like basketball or football, enjoys collecting his favorite athletic shoes and hats. He has a closet full of all kinds of sneakers.

"He has so many shoes," Bianca Bell said. "Piles of them. He's a maniac about shoes."

Nick Bell replied, "I just love to match (my clothes). The hats are just I thing I like."

"I'd love to be a coach someday," Bell said. "Maybe I could help with the school basketball team or something like that. I could really help by showing that you can work hard and win, even with cancer."

His experience has also given him opportunities to inform and educate. The Bell family, which has been involved in various cancer support and fund-raising efforts, has also established its own a children's cancer fund called, "Skipper's Angel Wings", to help other kids deal with the disease and the treatment.

"Dr. Aaron Raussen, Nick's doctor and a top oncologist at NYU, has had Nick speak to medical students about his experience with cancer and he's done a good job," Michélle Bell said. "I think his attitude and courage have helped him grow."

Young Nick is certain his "childhood" is over.

"I guess I was forced to grow up," Bell said. "Now I have to mature in school and get ready for college. I want to live a long life and do good things."

NINETEEN

A DOVE STORY

S OME BIRDS ARE symbols of uplifting and peace (the dove, the eagle) while others function as the Angel of Death (vultures, ravens).

On Mother's Day weekend 2014, a bird seemingly flew out of nowhere and landed on my doorstep in Bronxville, New York, My home was a small cozy, corner garden apartment where many neighbors walked past my door throughout the day, each day.

Kellye, a friend, noticed the bird standing next to my angel statue as she dropped me off after having dinner that rainy Friday night. She had noticed it earlier on when she had picked me up.

Kellye looked over at my porch, "Oh, my goodness, Michele, that white bird is still next to the statue from when I picked you up earlier."

I turned to her and said. "Oh My God, you're right! It's a sign, and you're the conduit to see the greater meaning."

"The bird is calling you through Spirit," Kellye said. "It's powerful, honey. He came to comfort you this weekend. This is how the other side can communicate with us."

I was in awe staring out the car window watching him through the raindrops as she talked to me about the bird. Thoughts were spinning in my head. *It's Mother's Day weekend. Is this yet another sign from my son? What message is he sending me now?*

"Kellye, thanks for dinner, but I have to build my bird a castle and get him some food!" I stepped out of her car and ran over to mine to drive to the Home Depot. Into my cart went tons of flowers, bird food, and some added bird decorations so he could feel at home.

That next morning, I woke up to begin my day of landscaping. The sun was shining bright, and guess who was on the windowsill looking through the screen? It was that faithful bird!

My mystical experience was still happening. I named him My Li'l Skipper. That was Nicky's nickname as a baby when he was dressed in his sailor outfit. We spent the whole day together, planting flowers, singing, and bonding. I felt divinely inspired. And often looked to my angel that Nicky had given me as I built Li'l Skipper a sanctuary.

On Sunday morning, Li'l Skipper was on the ledge again staring through the screen at me. As much as I did not want to leave this wondrous gift, my gut told me to let it go and be grateful for the time he was sent my way on such a delicate weekend.

Apparently, the neighbors were a bit taken back by the bird's presence and News 12 Westchester was at my door. The story made regional news. Reporters wanted the story, and I was more than happy to share, knowing that it would help someone else who was suffering, grieving.

As I packed to go back upstate to take care of my elderly mother, Li'l Skipper was pacing back and forth on the front steps

Occasionally, the bird would fly to a nearby tree and alight on a branch or perch on the roof of the four-story condo building, directly above my stoop, to keep his eye on my comings and goings.

That following week, I drove back downstate. As I was pulling up front, I could see Li'l Skipper perched up on the roof. I'd created a musical whistle that only he would recognize. As I approached the stairs whistling, he came swooping down inches above my head, strangely drawn to Nicky's broken ceramic angel near the doorstep.

Nicky's spirit was powerful. I believe his spirit is all around me—and the white bird is a manifestation of his spirit. The bird never left.

I took the drive down every weekend, staying long weekends. I would talk to the bird daily as if I was seeking out an answer. I knew there was a message that came with this gift, and it was time to spread my own wings and put it out there. That last and final weekend was Nicky's 26th birthday on June 20.

The night before I was heading back upstate, I moved my desk close enough to the window where I could write and be close to Li'l Skipper. I gathered my thoughts, poured a glass of wine, and placed a lit white candle on the glass table.

After darkness fell later in the evening, it was time to start talking to this bird.

Without hesitation, I leaned over near the screen, and I whispered gently, "My heart is heavy knowing you've held a constant vigil over me since Mother's Day. You've never left my side each time I came home. However, I know deep down I must let this place go in order to make a full sacrifice and commitment to take care of my mother. This is the hardest decision I have to make, and I need your help. So, tomorrow morning, when I wake up, I'll know the answer."

There's nothing more peaceful than waking up in a natural silence. I didn't hear the small chirps coming from the other room that morning. I lay in bed looking at the ceiling as if looking through all four units to the top of the roof, but I could not see my Li'l Skipper.

All of a sudden, I jumped out of bed using a mental positive visual of whatever was about to change. I knew I must move on for the betterment of what lay before me. I know that whatever sacrifice I made, I'd be rewarded with blessings.

The bird had left. He was nowhere to be seen as I walked outside singing and whistling to checked his food and water. At first, I thought someone had stolen him, but I took a breath in between the tears and reminded myself that this was a powerful message from beyond the grave.

Skeptics may scoff, but this is a true story.

Maybe it's a miracle, a message of some kind sent from on high. Or perhaps it is just "one of those things," a wonderful connection forged between a human being and a member of the natural world.

The protagonist is a mysterious bird — a pure, white dove.

(Photo: Submitted)

Seven days ago, the bird seemingly flew out of nowhere and landed at the doorstep of Michele Bell, a grieving mother who lives in a garden apartment at the corner of Bronxville Road and Texas Avenue in Yonkers, not far from where I live.

The bird never left.

Occasionally, the bird will fly to a nearby tree and alight on a branch or it will perch on the roof of the four-story apartment building, directly above Bell's stoop, and look down.

But always it returns to earth, strangely drawn to a broken ceramic angel that Bell keeps by the door.

The angel symbolizes Bell's son, Nicholas, who died in 2005 at age 18 of Ewing's sarcoma, a form of cancer that usually starts in a bone and mostly occurs in the teenage years.

Nick Bell was a brave young man whose fight for life, a four-year ordeal that included an arduous regimen of radiation treatments and chemotherapy, was chronicled by this newspaper. He had hoped to write an inspirational book about his experiences to help other sick kids, but he never got that chance.

"My relationship with my son was so beautiful," Bell said on a recent day, fighting back tears. "We had such a strong, unconditional love, the love that transcends death."

During Nick's long and painful struggle, his family formed a children's cancer fund called "Skipper's Angel Wings." Nick was given the nickname Skipper as a baby when he was dressed in a sailor outfit.

"He was really loved by so many people," his mother said. "You know, his spirit was powerful and he was so faithful."

Bell believes that Nick's spirit is all around her — and that the white bird is a manifestation of his spirit. She aptly named the bird Skipper.

The feathered friend arrived at Bell's home over Mother's Day weekend, after Bell had had an especially difficult time dealing with her mother, who was diagnosed with dementia. Bell recalled that the bird went straight to the ceramic angel.

"And the bird is out there, perched on that little cement thing next to the statue and it was raining," she said. "The bird just stayed there. So peaceful."

She values the bird's steadfastness, and encourages its loyalty by providing water and bird seed.

She sings and talks to it. Sometimes it seems as if the bird listens and understands. At night, it sleeps on her windowsill.

"Every day I'm astounded," Bell said. "He doesn't leave."

If the bird is lost, she would like to return it to its owner. But she said if no one comes forth, "then he was meant to be here for a reason."

Bell has had a hard-luck life, harder than most. When Nick was sick, she was fired from her job. She always suspected that it was in retaliation for missing work to tend to her son. A single mother, she quickly became short of money and lost her home in Tuckahoe.

Story by Phil Reisman

Today, she is getting back on her feet. Things are beginning to look up. She is engaged. And she has a daughter, Bianca, who loves her, and two grandchildren.

When I visited her one day this week, she was standing in front of her home. The white bird was there, too.

Bell talked about her life. Mostly she talked about her lost boy.

"Eighteen years — they went by in a blink," she said.

She told me about her son's courage and about his last birthday party, which was held in grand style at the VIP Country Club in New Rochelle. They went together, like prom dates. "You and Me Against the World" — that's the song they sang together.

Nick died six months later, in his own bed, surrounded by his family.

His last words were, "Mom, I'm going home."

Determined to make something good come from tragedy.
"Adopt a Family" Pick an Angel" were just a few programs
offered to families facing a childhood terminal illness.

Skipper's Angel Wings auction a huge success

Skipper's Angel Wings, a local support group that helps families whose children are dealing with cancer, received some strong community support last week when it held its Bachelor and Bachelorette Auction fund-raiser at Sweet Caroline's restaurant in Eastchester.

"Goumba Johnny", the morning host on WSTU radio (103.5 FM) and a New Rochelle resident, was a surprise guest bachelor who brought in $450.

"We had wonderful help from a number of local businesses and even though we didn't raise as much as we did the first time we held the auction, it was a good event," said Skipper's organizer Michele Bell.

Giovanni's Deli, Pizza Mia, Candace Hair, Kim's Nails, Starbucks, Tano's Jewelry, Solar Eclipse, Phoenix Fitness, Reiner Kitchens, Trader Joe's, Baskets and More, Century Drugs, Michael's Flora Craft and Adriana Spa donated gifts for the event's raffle.

Tom Farley and his legal office team of Mary Beth Mullins and Tom Brundidge helped contribute $1,600 to Skipper's.

"We want to thank volunteers Jackie Perretti, Laura Boezi, Joy Greuce and Annmarie DiChiarian and Sweet Caroline's for all their help in getting the event together," Bell said.

— Danny Lagiera

Photos by Angela Gaul/Review Press

Above. Extenie, a stand-up comedian from Manhattan who goes solely by his first name, auctions off a date with Ken Cook, of Mount Vernon, during a charity event at Sweet Caroline's in Eastchester Nov. 6. The bachelor/bachelorette auction was a fund-raiser for Skipper's Angel Wings, a not-for-profit organization that supports children with cancer and their families.
Left, Shiva Zanoll, left, and Gloria Vinelli, both of White Plains, clap and cheer as their friend MaryBeth Mullins participates in the bachelorette auction at Sweet Caroline's. Bidders drove the price of a date with Mullins up to approximately $300.

Angels for a day

Louis De Chiarro of New Rochelle styles the hair of Barbara Feyl, grandmother of Skipper. Barbara Feyl visited from Troy, New York for the day to support the event. Text/Photos by Linda Barat

The Louis De Chiarro Salon in Eastchester donated all proceeds from its salon services for the day on May 1 to Skippers Angel Wings Children's Cancer Fund. The fund, based in Eastchester, helps families of children with cancer.

Lisa Blanco of Bronxville, Nicolas "Skipper" and Michele Bell, and Edye Marchese, all of Eastchester.

Saundra Reed works on Gail Perrotta of Eastchester during Sunday's fundraiser for children with cancer.

A hair-raising fundraiser

Group that 'adopts' families with cancer has day at beauty salon

Mary Iarocci
For the Review Press

Hairstylist Saundra Reed asked clients to schedule appointments at the Louis De Chiaro Salon to raise money for children with cancer.

Within two days her appointment book was full.

"There was no hesitation," Reed said. "Clients just booked."

Proceeds of the fundraiser went to Skipper's Angel Wings, a non-profit organization founded by Michelle Bell after her son Nick was diagnosed with cancer in 2002.

The group aims to assist families with teen, un-health care bills and transportation costs associated with cancer treatment.

Bell said the staff of the Eastchester salon volunteered their services for the May 1 fundraiser. Stickers, raffles for salon gift certificates and bubble bath were sold to raise additional funds.

"The salon is packed. They've dedicated themselves to helping us move forward with our mission," she said.

Clients were given scalp favors and offered food and wine while getting their hair done.

Richard Randig is a practitioner of reiki, a Japanese stress-reduction technique that promotes healing. He offered his services at the salon for the day.

"It's a nice introduction to the salon and their clients," Randig said, adding that profits would benefit "a good cause."

'Skipper'

Nick Bell, 17, acquired the nickname "Skipper" as a baby when his mother put him in a skipper's outfit. The organization named after him has "adopted" four families since its beginning.

Michelle Bell formed the organization to provide assistance to families struggling with cancer. The single mother lost her job and her home when her son was diagnosed with bone cancer — Ewing's sarcoma — at 14.

"I don't want to see other families go through what I went through," Bell said.

"I'm proud of my mother. She does a lot for families," Nick Bell said.

Nick Bell recently stopped chemotherapy and has been taking food supplement glyconutrients for six weeks.

"I'm on the nutrients, and I feel fine," he said.

Lisa G. Bianco dressed in an an-

gel costume and stood outside the salon next to a table of brochures. She sold stickers and raffle tickets for a gift certificate to the salon and handed out information about glyconutrients.

"Glyconutrients do not cure conditions. The necessary sugars help the cells and the immune system identify what they need. As a result, it can take care of chronic conditions," Bianco said.

Bianco said she suffered from multiple chronic conditions for 15 years, including migraines and high blood pressure. She said since taking glyconutrients, she has not been sick in four and a half years.

Reed has been involved with Locks of Love, an organization that donates hair to cancer patients, for three years. Her clients at MSalon in Manhattan contributed $270 toward the May 1 fundraiser in Eastchester.

"It just shows how wonderful people are," Reed said. "For us to donate this day is so worth it."

"For the first time doing this, I was a little afraid," said owner Louis De Chiaro of opening the salon on a Sunday to hold the fundraiser. However, he said the event was a success.

Reed thanked all those who participated.

"The community really supported us. We have great clientele," Reed said. "I love what I do."

4-15-2005

Taxi taking extra fares in wake of Bus strike — p. 12

The Town Report

A weekly newspaper serving Eastchester, Bronxville and Tuckahoe

'A Lighter Day' of Beauty for Skipper's Angel Wings

By Alex Malecki
EASTCHESTER

"But if you can make it through the night, there will be a lighter day," wrote Martha Bell to his mother Michelle this past Christmas. That is what Nicky, who will suffer the Bell, wings becomes (a bone cancer) and his mother are working toward a lighter day. On Sunday, May 1, the Louis DeChiaro Salon in 14 Mill Road in Eastchester will host "A Day of Beauty" for Skipper's Angel Wings, the foundation Bell started to aid families who are experiencing what — see Skipper page 9

EPILOGUE

A FEW MONTHS before Nicky came home from the hospital, he lay in his bed, propped up, and staring up at the ceiling, with his hands folded in prayer across his chest. I was at his bedside, holding his hand.

Looking at him with tears in the brims of my eyes, I asked, "Nicky, what are you thinking about, sweetheart?"

His voice crackled, "Ma, I'm dying. I'll never be able to live to experience what I had hoped for." And for a moment, there was silence before he went on, "Basketball, college, a family, watching my children play in the yard, and a wife who would be a lot like you, Mom."

How could this precious gift I prayed for leave my life?

There is no answer.

There are things that we don't want to happen. However, we have to accept things we don't want to know, but we need to learn, and there are people we can't live without, but we have to release them. The story of my life has many chapters. One bad chapter doesn't mean it's the end. So, I needed to stop re-reading the bad one and turn the page. The path to unconditional happiness comes from deep personal transformation. I must own who I am and come to peace with pain. Remember, life does not have to be anywhere near perfect to be wonderful in the end. Most importantly, forgive others, not because they deserve forgiveness, but because we deserve peace. Faith forward. Live authentic.

NOTES & THOUGHTS

I catch myself sometimes as I whisper to my son, feeling his presence next to me.

Dear Nick,

Your death has been my greatest teacher. I could have shut down, instead I opened my heart to receive the unconditional love you left with me the eve of your transition into the light. Your death woke me up. Released my fears to embrace my grief and empower me with a voice I can't ignore.

My grief has not changed me, it has revealed me.

"I miss our slumber parties, our late night movies, listening to your dreams, taking pictures with our cell phones, and holding you in my arms throughout the night with my head on your shoulder.

"Most of all, I miss how you would kiss me on the forehead every single time you went to bed or left the house. You never missed a beat! Your heart was huge, and you were such a grateful son. Even during your final moments before God took you home, you were always thinking of others.

"I am at peace knowing that you are safe, and that one day, I will see you again. I feel and know that you are always around me, helping me attain the strength I need to get through another day. I talk about you all the time, even to strangers I meet. When I speak about you, it is no longer with tears, but with tremendous pride.

"That doesn't mean I never cry, but that my pride for you has overtaken my need for my own selfish and public tears.

"Yes, if I could say something to you now, as you are on the other side, I would say, 'Nicky, you were and still are everything a mother could ever wish for in a son. I love and miss you and as long as I breathe, I'll keep your memory alive'.

"When I conceived you, I wished and prayed to God every night that you'd be a remarkable child and, thankfully, you were. Come closer, Nicky, and I'll tell you a little secret—you still are a remarkable child!"

∞

UNDERNEATH MY SMILE or silliness, my heart suffers so much. I sometimes feel it'll never heal. I will never hear *yohimu* laugh or see that beautiful smile again.

Months passed, and I grieved quietly, alone. I thought the dates on the calendar, once so important, were no longer so because I could not share them with him. The daily routines became so mundane.

Everything reminded me of Nicky, and I found no escape, the pain flowing through my veins. It sears my soul to even remember that first year.

My first Mother's Day was emblazoned by questions: How do I live life more fully? Where do I begin to embrace the meaning of life? How did my child adapt to the capacity of living his life while on the edge of death?

I talked to him in my mind: You're no longer here on earth, where we look upon one another with animosity, jealousy, judgment or even hatred. You're now in a place that's truly loving and free of pain. You tried your hardest to be the peacemaker, but more importantly, your behavior displayed the soul of a true man with an honest heart.

The heavy blanket lifted slowly, and now the deep sadness no longer exists. My heart knows Nicky's safe where he is. I still tell him, in my heart, *You are more alive than ever, working in heaven and watching over Mommy.*

I tell him, It became more apparent through our sick journey that the purpose of life is to learn to appreciate all the various aspects of ourselves. Through life's ups and downs. You grew in knowledge and wisdom and accomplished this in a very short, yet quite complete, life.

I always smiled when I saw his face and laughed when I felt like crying. I always let him choose his clothes and smiled when I saw how perfect those choices were. I always stepped over my laundry to pick him up and take him to the park.

I always left the dishes in the sink to watch Nicky play his favorite sports. He taught me how to spend precious moments of quality, loving time together. We would blow bubbles in the backyard, and I'd never yell or grumble when he screamed because the ice cream truck came by.

I never worried about where Nicky went out to or who he went with. I never second-guessed those decisions. He had to have two Happy Meals from McDonald's so he could have both toys: one for him and one for his sister.

He was beyond thoughtful of others.

∞

WHENEVER I KISSED Nicky goodnight and gave him a squeeze, tighter and tighter, I thanked God and asked Him for nothing except for one more day with him.

Now with him gone, loneliness fills me, whether I'm asleep or awake.

∞

IF YOU'RE GOING through a similar tragedy, find a friend, confidant or fellow survivor. I've found that people in our tribe want to help us in our times of need.

Take the time for those near and dear to you, for tomorrow is never promised us. I encourage grieving souls not to let guilt and shame define who you are. Get off your phones and computers, and consistently spend quality time with your loved ones.

There will be times you'll be angry and sad, but try to keep calm, and pray for patience. There's nothing more meaningful than showing deep love to a child who's fighting for his or her life.

Beautiful people do not just happen.

The most beautiful people we have known are those who have known defeat, known suffering, known struggle, known loss, and have found their way out of the depths. These people have an appreciation, sensitivity and an understanding of life that fills them with compassion, gentleness, and deep, loving concern.

When someone you love dies, you realize for the first time what life is all about. You begin to see that your life here is nothing but the sum total of every choice you have made during each moment of your life. Your thoughts, which you are responsible for, are as real as your deeds. You will begin to realize that every thought, word, and deed affects your life and has also touched thousands of lives.

—Dr. Elisabeth Kübler-Ross.
Used by permission of The Elisabeth Kübler-Ross Family Limited Partnership

∞

A COUPLE OF years after Nicky passed away, I returned to our house where he left his body. I knocked on the door hoping whoever was home would answer. A young guy came to the porch. And after I explained why I was there, he was nice enough to let me in. Of course, the surroundings were not the same. I knew my son wasn't there, but subconsciously, I was looking for him. I cried a little and then left. I'd found what I was looking for.

As I walked back to my car, I thought of the many parents who lose their children without having the opportunity to say goodbye. I was blessed to have had that opportunity. The days leading up to his last breath were challenging. I walked on eggshells feeling each moment of his anxiety, sadness, and pain. How could I encourage his heart to keep fighting when I knew deep down inside that he was tired as he hung on to the raw reality of his illness?

How does a grieving mother express happiness? We diminish our wants and augment our means. Society encourages us to appreciate what you have and then to long for those things which are gone. At this writing, nearly a dozen years on, there's always a plan. And my soul knows what it is.

Nicky taught me the most important lesson of all—that our riches are always found within.

Today, caring for my mother in upstate New York is frustrating. I am now reliving the very same emotions with her care, at the very same time of year, watching dementia take over her body. I've returned to my hometown to take care of my mother, after living a life of twenty-plus years away.

Observing this disease daily that has taken over my mother's brain is a slow transition into her next life—a certainty that wisdom can be attained as I am forced to pay attention knowing the connection we never had, and is now mending, matters to me deeply. We must love unconditionally while we can.

My son taught me another most important lesson, that our riches are found within. When your heart is ripped open with a loss, grief creates ebb and flow as the current of grief *will reveal you.*

My soul craves the passions of living and breathing, but also about preparing myself for the moment "until we meet again."

Finally reaching *acceptance*, currently living in *authentic grief* and learning about the five stages of grief (by <u>Elisabeth Kubler-Ross)</u>, I was now ready to journey into my own theme of grief stages that saved me. I mean SAVED me.

The 7 Stages of Grief ***ALIGNMENT...***

E M B R A C E

Living with Intent

Express - Emotional Journaling: A journal acts as a free talk therapist..."someone" you can spill all your feelings to, no matter what, without judgment. Getting your emotions down on paper can help you to process difficult times as well as help you with sorting out general emotional difficulty. Using a journal to self-express can relieve anxiety, help you to understand negative emotional triggers, and resolve problems in your daily life.

Meditate - When we connect to our breathing consciously, we connect to the present moment. Quite your mind to tap into your deepest intentions: be open to receive the messages the universe sends you -- and allow that knowledge to guide you.

Be Present - Put down the balls you're juggling for a moment. Let's embrace the beauty of mono-tasking. The act of being present is, in a sense, a meditation without meditating. Stillness comes from action - breathing, attending, witnessing, releasing and breathing again. This simple cycle can profoundly change the way that we experience our world. Mindful living will help connect you to your life purpose.

Rejuvenate - Disconnect. Reassess your life. Get away on a day trip. Pamper yourself. Cleanse. Yoga Dance. Declutter your home. Schedule time for a divine self care ritual in the morning and evening. Create a vision board. Do nothing.

Awaken - Turn your attention inward and observe yourself, placing your attention firmly in the present moment. The NOW. Be mindful of your thoughts, analyze your feelings, pay attention to the sensations in your body, feel your breath. Engage in self-examination, and survey your situation and surroundings from a higher perspective. The goal is to retrieve what was locked away within us, to re-establish contact with our higher centers, and ultimately remember who we are. And it all begins with self-observation and listening to your heart.

Connect - Self-compassion: Take 20 minutes daily to honor our bodies, our minds, and our spirit. **Adopt an attitude of gratitude.** In giving thanks my blessings will multiply. When we focus on gratitude, we teach our brains to look for positive things in our world. **Be still.** Meditation is medicine for the mind and healing for the soul. In meditation, we allow stillness of our minds, and this is how we connect to inspiration.

Eat Healthy - Mindful eating also known as intuitive eating aims to reconnect us more deeply with the experience of eating. Enjoying our food is what we are after. Here are some examples:

- **Know Your Food:** Considering the health value on your shopping list. Fill most of your cart with the produce section and avoid center aisles and check-out counter.
- **Savor the Silence:** Reflect with gratitude before you begin eating. Silence phones. Shut off the TV. Focus on "how" you eat, not what is around you while you eat.

- **Savor the Flavor:** *Smell. Chew.* Taste. Bring all your senses to the meal. Take time to enjoy the flavors and textures. Chew 25 times to prevent overeating.
- **Small portions:** Limit the size of your plate to 9 inches or less. Smaller plates will help you with portion control. You crave less if you see less.
- **Utensil Release:** Putting down your utensils between bites will allow you to enjoy what you already have in your mouth.

And so to EMBRACE the lesson of grief is to remember them with "more love", By purposely aligning your grief with these above methods, they can be mentally healthy during the process of dealing with a significant loss.

SPECIAL TRIBUTE STORY

WRITTEN BY A special friend I met during the Solstice Moon on June 20, 2016, just hours after my Unalome tattoo. During a yoga dance, the instructor asked us to choose a partner to create a story through music. The energy was intense throughout. Tears flowed between us without words spoken. After the dance completed, our hands joined exchanging names.

"Hi, I'm Barbara."

"It's such a pleasure to meet you. I'm Michele. My mother's name is Barbara." Our hands did not let loose. There was still a much stronger connection about to release, and we were both ready to receive.

"My daughter's name is Michele. You wouldn't happen to have a son named Daniel?"

"No, actually, my son's name is Nicky, and I'm here celebrating his twenty-ninth birthday this week. He's no longer with us."

Barbara added, "I lost my son two years ago."

At that moment, we both felt the powerful Divine intervention and energy. Two mothers brought together to share their story of love, loss, and life moving forward.

Here is Barbara's story.

A Mother's Day Gift from Beyond
By Barbara D. Pastie

Where does one even begin to tell the story of losing a son? Does one focus on the moment of death? Or on the beginning of life? Or all the years in between? Does one discuss the tragedy and the grief? Or the love and the miracles?

I'll start with four months before the end. My son, Daniel, was 38 years old when Mother's Day, 2013 came around. Daniel's love of farming from an early age led him to a degree in Animal Science and a career in Agriculture. As the Vice President of Marketing and Business Development for Dairylea in Syracuse, NY, he traveled extensively across the country assisting farmers and farm supply companies in obtaining the best equipment possible for their customers and their farms.

He came to be known as "that guy who knows everything about farming."

Health-wise, Daniel had his challenges. He suffered from stenosis of the spine and misalignment in his skeleton. By his mid-30's he had already had two surgeries for herniated discs as well as a total hip replacement. He suffered terribly from the stenosis and had several very painful but temporary treatments to kill the nerves to his back. Doctors were reluctant to fuse his spine due to his young age. His biggest fear was that he would end up in a wheelchair. Despite the pain, he continued to work but was limited in participating in the sports he loved, such as golf and hiking.

So on the Friday prior to Mother's Day, I was surprised to find Daniel at my door with a beautiful vase of flowers. I knew he had just returned from a business trip and he must be in pain. He landed at the airport in Syracuse and then drove three hours to Pittsfield to surprise me for Mother's Day. Despite his pain, he was determined to celebrate with me. But he wanted me to understand we would have to have dinner early Saturday so he could drive back home and ice his back all-day Sunday in order to return to work.

I was so touched by his love and devotion, and I counted my blessings. It was the last Mother's Day I would see him alive.

Three months later, on August 5, 2013, my husband, Paul, and I received the call which every parent has nightmares about. Daniel had collapsed at work, was unresponsive, and had been rushed to the hospital. We needed to get there at once. And my daughter, Michelle, who lived in Florida, had to fly home. I would need to write a book of my own to describe the month to follow—the terror, the decisions, the love, the miracles—and the end. Daniel suffered a subarachnoid hemorrhage (a brain aneurysm).

It was only the rapid response of his co-workers who were trained EMTs and the providence that brought him to Upstate University Hospital in Syracuse,

NY, that kept him alive. He had the best doctors and nurses possible, but his prospects were never hopeful, and we thought we would lose him more than once. Ultimately, Paul and I, as his next of kin, had to make the most horrible and gut-wrenching decision of our lives—to stop all extraordinary measures and, barring a miracle, let him go. We knew with all our hearts that he would never want a life that was less than whole.

By another miracle, we were able to move Daniel to Francis House in Syracuse, NY where he transitioned with dignity and love on September 6, 2013, with me by his side. (Everyone else had gone out. I was alone with him when he died, which is one of the greatest blessings of my life.)

By now you must be wondering, "How did Daniel manage to send you flowers for Mother's Day in 2014?" Well, because I told him to! I had a little talk with him prior to Mother's Day. "Daniel," I said, "You have to send me flowers for Mother's Day again this year. And they can't be from your father or your sister. They have to come from somewhere I'm not expecting." I didn't tell anyone about my request.

On the Friday before Mother's Day, Paul and I were having breakfast when there was a knock at the back door. When I opened it, there stood the neighbor who owns a florist business (she did all the lovely flowers for Dan's funeral), with a gorgeous flower arrangement. "Are those from my daughter?" I asked.

"No," she replied. "You'll have to look at the card." The flowers were sent by Dan's dearest friends, Jennifer, Cameron, and Tony, who had supported us throughout his illness, served as pallbearers and showered us with love. But I knew who had really sent the flowers.

Later, when I thanked Jennifer, she told me the story. The week before Mother's Day she said she had an overwhelming urge to send me flowers. She immediately contacted Cam and Tony, and all three of them pitched in to get the flowers. And she, too, knew who had really sent the flowers.

So that's how I got my "flowers from beyond." There are many more stories and many more miracles. Daniel's life (and suffering and death) had purpose and meaning. And now, even though he is gone from this life, he continues to show us love and humor and an assurance that there is more than this physical plane. And every so often, he finds ways to let us know he is still around.

NICK'S MYSPACE

N OW, EVERYONE REMEMBERS MySpace. It was actually the largest social networking site in the world. A popular social network among teenagers and young adults.

In his My Space Blurb, here is what he wrote in his exact verbiage and typeset.

About Me:

to live u gotta have balls, got to have balls in this "WORLD" or u aint goin nowhere... its too deep, u cant get on my level even if u tried too, even if they started teachin it in school... u still wouldnt be on my Level u could never be like me or think like me, nawwh not u... not u...your not me patnah... n im not u... been through sum shit and seen a lot of things, so my life my friends my family and my dreams are swept away, seeing best friends almost a brother to me... Lie there mumble and he can't even say a word to me just as big eyes bulging looking at me trying to push that one word out, barely moving stuck in one position for two months and a day not able to speak or move in pain for two months there's nothing we could do second option would just to pull the plug but with faith and not seeing him for days that one on the ninth floor NYU medical center I remember so many memories stomach getting nauseous mouth started to water I can't walk in there premeditated thoughts... Suck it up see your boy... And I'm glad I did what I see Mikey up watching football talking shit and looking great as can be, just like old times, when the doc said it didn't look like we had a disease, this shit can't beat us - boy boy - we warriors, we fighters til the end, ain't nothin stopping us... neva get them years back, u can pray all u want, moments can be so precious, but only remembered in memory...the worse can get worse, and turn around in a blink of an eye, doubled the times...can neva get them bak no matter how hard u try, this "WORLD" we live in is fuked up, it's really fuked up, I got their blueprint in my head- n wut their tryin to do is greasy people-if u only knew wut the life we live is all about...if everything wasn't so commercialized, and people werent so corrupted n selfish, maybe things wud be better...Nawh i dont think so... "money is the root of all EVIL" its a chain of evil, and planned out decisions...maybe this is the pearly gates n people take advantage and God puts them in place, kinda like karma, that's why so many things happen... n what if hell is a million times worse then wut we live today, is there heaven and hell? is there even a God? ... is there even saints, wut if this book called the "Bible" is a book sumone wrote on a drug trip, we may never know, wut if the rumor spread about all this, and people just believe wut they hear...? questions? FAITH...<~~~~answer(bang)...enough said....EXCELLENCE!!! otha than that, im an all around guy haha, can keep a conversation goin, likes to have fun, too much fun...im down for anything... im not like evry guy or kidd on here... I consider myself a man, I dont do that high school drama kaka, im not lookin for anybody on MySpace, because its impossible to meet somebody on here that wont waste ur time...every girl on here is the same, ive seen too many guidettes on MySpace more than ive seen in my lifetime, that shit plays out cuzzy...im here to make friends, and show myself off, im not cocky, im confident, you dont like it, u think I give a fuk" nawwh...theres only ONE thing in this world u can TRUST, and its YOU, you kno everything that goes on wit anything, just keep them lips sealed "Loose Lips Sink Ships" just an example ST MAARTEN, my home away from home-Italy ill be comin home soon...

Nicky Bell

Danielle and Danielle

Playing in the sands of the Caribbean

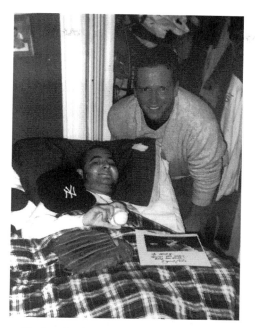

Yankee Pitcher, David Cone visits Nick

His friends gather on our porch to say goodbye
that dreadful eve of 12-29-2005

Last Holiday at the mall shopping with his friends one week before he transitioned. He makes a peace sign to his friends.

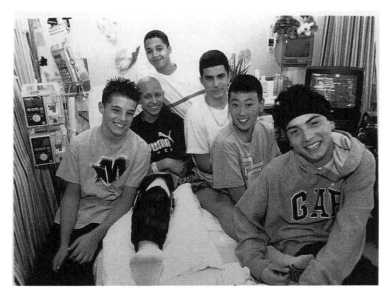

Best friends remain on his cancer journey til the end

Unbeknownst to Nicky his dreams were about
to be shattered that fateful day

Meet and Greet with Shaquille O'Neal

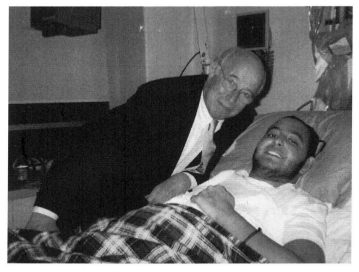

Dr. Aaron Rausen and team of devoted nurses at NYU

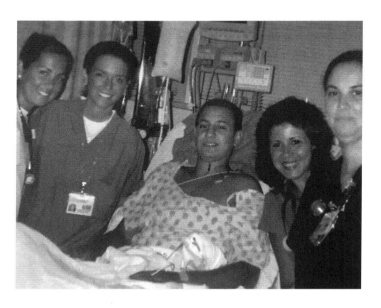

Clubbing with friends

Egg McMuffin and beer at McDonalds in France

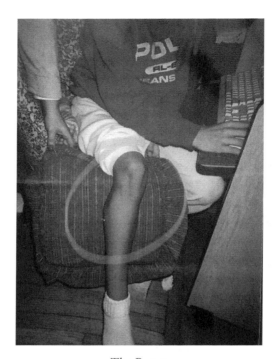

The Bump

Rock Climbing with his leg brace in the Bahamas

Playing golf at the TPC in Arizona

Ice hockey was one of his favorite winter sports

NICKY'S SPIRIT LIVES ON

A Note from Nicky's Babysitter

FROM THE MOMENT I met Nicky, he he smiled—a perfect, genuine smile. I started out as his sister's cheerleading coach, and then I became their babysitter. Both kids were great. I never had a difficult time caring for either of them. We spent many hours, days, and nights together, and they truly became a part of my life.

Nicky was handsome. Black hair, dark eyes, and an olive complexion, accompanied by a smile and personality impressive for a nine-year-old. He was respectful, easygoing, and happy. Nothing much triggered him to be sad or angry.

One thing I always admired, and still reflect upon to this day, is the unconditional love he had for his mother. She could do no wrong. He never gave her a difficult time. He was the 'perfect son.'

For a while, I lost touch with the Bell family. As the kids grew older, they started to have more interests in friends, and they were old enough to care for themselves. Then I found out Nicky was sick and fighting cancer. A part of me was in complete shock. I thought it was a rumor and didn't want to know otherwise. But, when I realized it wasn't, my heart dropped, and I needed to be in touch with them again.

I contacted Michele, Nicky's mother. She knew I wanted to see Nicky. That's when I finally realized the gravity of his illness. And yet, when I first saw him, he smiled. I wasn't surprised because that was Nicky—happy, grateful, and strong. As time went by, he had good days and great moments, such as the surprise birthday bash his mother threw for him on his eighteenth birthday. He looked so handsome in his photos. I prayed that his cancer would go away and that he would spend a lifetime with his family.

However, some prayers aren't answered.

One day, I received a call that Nicky was not doing well. Nicky said he was 'going home,' which meant heaven. Nicky knew where he belonged. He fought until the end with dignity, like a man well beyond his years. I couldn't imagine how Michele, his sister, his father or grandmother could continue after this loss. But now, I see that this angel, who was once here, is in heaven watching over us. With all he had gone through, it makes sense that he was here to touch the lives of everyone in a sweet, good-hearted way. Whenever I see Michele, she's strong, positive, and she still strives to live a good life—despite her incredible loss.

It hurts to think that he's not physically here anymore, but it's beautiful and inspiring to remember who Nicky was during the short time God loaned him to us. It's amazing how much one can learn from a child's grace. I know Nicky's spirit lives on in Michele's heart. It was pure pleasure to share some days with her angel.

Thank you, Michele, and thank you, Nicky!

— Rosa Lage

ACKNOWLEDGMENTS

A DEEP BOW of gratitude to God, who is now in possession of my son.

For their love, support and assistance, goes out to the late Dr. Aaron Rausen; my mother, Barbara, for all of her prayers and devoted Catholicism, as well as her two-hour trips to frequently visit from upstate New York at an advanced age; all of the medical staff on 9 East at NYU who quickly became family; the Make-A-Wish Foundation; devoted friends of Nicky. I am humbled by your love and dedication.

A special expression of gratitude to Renzo --- your tireless support, encouragement and love are a gift beyond measure.

I would also like to thank Yankee player David Cone, Shaquille O'Neal, Vida Guerra, and many more; my Higher Power, for giving me the strength to endure, find peace within my soul, and new-found friendships; a special thank you to Dianne Gray and the Elisabeth-Kubler Ross Foundation for their gracious support. Gianna, Dante, Gabriella and Chazz Palminteri for always having an open ear, continued friendship, and who opened their hearts to my story.

Sincere heartfelt gratitude to the many friends who have remained on my spiritual grief journey all these years. To my colleagues who have read this book in its many forms, I offer my never ending thanks through your guidance as I struggled to rebirth my baby.

To the families currently suffering within - no matter how big or small, always know my heart is with you always. Friends Of Karen,

Cancer Care, National Child's Cancer Society, and the Spano family for your willingness to offer support was a true blessing. My girls, Laura, Barbara and Tamara for sharing your stories in our book- the serendipity of how life brought us together is forever cherished.

And, to the Weaver family in Texas: Kenneth (Kenny), Rosemarie (Rosy), Melissa, Michelle and Melinda Weaver. You will be eternally remembered for your courage and strength. Sharing your story with the world has changed millions of lives. For the gift you gave to all of us. For that, and so much more, I'm forever blessed.

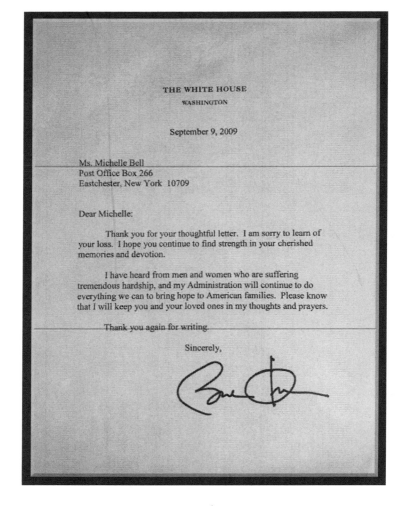

THE WHITE HOUSE
WASHINGTON

September 9, 2009

Ms. Michelle Bell
Post Office Box 266
Eastchester, New York 10709

Dear Michelle:

Thank you for your thoughtful letter. I am sorry to learn of your loss. I hope you continue to find strength in your cherished memories and devotion.

I have heard from men and women who are suffering tremendous hardship, and my Administration will continue to do everything we can to bring hope to American families. Please know that I will keep you and your loved ones in my thoughts and prayers.

Thank you again for writing.

Sincerely,

11
The Mystical Number

In our story you just read, I spoke briefly about a Life Path 11. As our book was in the design stages before we published, I shared with a few people the impact of how the number 11 has been engaging within my journey in the last few years.

My goal was to publish my book on 12-29-2017 which is Nicky's Heavenly anniversary. As the Divine Universe gently guided the release, it is only by the grace of the powers-that-be we were set for a 2018 release.

Simply Serendipitously Explained

My Life Path number is **11** (Found out 3
years ago about numerology)
It took me **11** years to complete our book
Launched in 2018
2+0+1+8= **11**

All of which add up to the number **33**

Nicky's Life Path number is a **33**

M A G I C A L

This is the storybook I made for Nicky a few months before he transitioned. This storybook will be made into a chapbook one day.

This is A story
  ABOUT
   " *Life* "

AND windstorms, About
SEEDS that we plant in the
SPRING, AND flowers that bloom
in the summer And harvest
in the fall.

   " *DEATH* "

that COMES EARLY in Life
AND to some people late
AND what it is ALL ABOut

Imagine the very
beginning of Life and
God who created everything-
As the sun shines all over
the world And
warms us. The sun
makes the flowers
grow and the
warm rays that
cover the earth-
even when clouds
make it impossible
for us to see them.

God Always sees us, his love
Always shines on us And it
does not matter how small
or how big we are and
nothing can ever
Stop that!

When people are born, they start out as tiny seeds like the dandelion seeds that are blown into the meadow - Some end up in the gutter, or a pretty lawn in front of the fairy mansion, some on a flower bed -

And so it is with us, we start our life in a rich home or poor family, or an orphanage or beloved by parents who wanted us very much like you Nicky, we wanted you very much!

Some people may call this
the "Gamble of Life"
but you must remember that
God is also in charge of the wind
and He cares as much about
dandelion seeds as He cares for
all living things —
    Especially children - and there
are no coincedences in Life!

    He never discriminates, He loves
unconditionally, He understands,
He does not judge - He is all Love
    You and God picked your own
parents out of a choice of a billion

    You chose them
    so you can help
    them grow and learn
    as they are your teacher
    too

Life is like a school where we are
given a chance to learn many
things – like to get along with other
people, or to understand our
feelings, to learn to be honest
with ourselves and others – to
learn to give and receive love –
And when we have passed all
the tests – (just like in school)
we are allowed to graduate –
that means we are all allowed
to return to our "Real Home"
to God where we all came from
and where we meet all the
people we ever loved – or missed
in our life prior to here.
– That is the time when we
die, when we shed our body,
when we have done our work
and are able to move on.

Winter

Spring

Summer

Fall

In the winter you cannot
see life in a tree - - - -

But when Spring comes, the
small green leaves come out
on after another - - - -

And in late summer the tree
is full of fruit and has
fullfilled its promise, it's
mission and purpose.

In the fall the leaves fall
off - one by one and the
tree goes to "Rest" over
winter

♥ Some flowers bloom
only for a few days—
EVERY body admires them
& loves them as a sign of ♥
SPRING AND HOPE.

Then they die — but
they have done what they
needed to do!
Some flowers bloom for A
very long time — people
take them for granted,
don't even notice them
Any more — the way they
treat old people — they
watch them sitting in a
Park until they are gone
forever

WINTER | SPRING

FALL | SUMMER

DAY

NIGHT

SPIRITUAL (GOD) | INTELLECTUAL (THINKING)

MAN

EMOTIONAL (FEELING) | PHYSICAL (BODY)

Everything in life is
a circle; Day follows
Night, spring comes
After winter.

When a boat disappears
behind the horizon, it is
Not "gone", just out of sight.

God watches over
everything that He created
the earth, the sun, the trees,
flowers and people ---
who have to get through
the "School of Life"
before they graduate.

When we have done all the work we were sent to earth to do - we are allowed to shed our body - which imprisons our soul like a cocoon encloses the future butterfly - - - AND when the time is right we can let go of it and we will be free of pain, free of fears and worries... free as a very beautiful BUTTERFLY, RETURNING home to GOD.

Which is A PLACE where we are never alone - where we continue to grow, sing + dance, where we are with those we loved (who shed their cocoons EARLIER) AND where we are surrounded with MORE LOVE than you can ever IMAGINE!

Remembered on the hardwood

Friends and family pay tribute to the life of Nick Bell

By John Miele

Friday, March 3, 2006.

It was a night that the late Nick Bell would have been proud to have seen, as all of his friends paid tribute to him on the basketball court at Eastchester High School. With everyone bringing a competitive edge and a chance to shed a tear on the hardwood, his friends and family found comfort to see the impact that Nick made on his local community.

Jacqueline Rank believed that Nick's memory felt the need to be preserved and she did so with a night of basketball.

Nick Bell passed away after a five-year battle with bone cancer - Ewing's sarcoma on Dec. 29, 2005.

"Nick got cancer from playing basketball," said Rank. "Even after he got

see Nick Bell page 15

Nick Bell would have been proud to see his friends and family pay tribute to his legacy.

Nicola Bell, 18, dies; Tuckahoe teen fought 4-year cancer battle

Mother had begun group for families living with the disease

Hope Salley
Review Press

Tuckahoe resident Nicola F. Bell died Dec. 29, after a four-year struggle with cancer. He was 18 years old.

Bell was diagnosed with cancer in 2002. In March, he chose to stop chemotherapy and instead take food

Nicola Bell

supplement gly-conutrients — sugars to help his immune system.

"Nicky," as he was known by family and friends, was courageous during his battle with the disease, according to his mother, Michele Bell. She formed a non-profit organization, called Skipper's Angel Wings, in his honor.

"Every minute of his life was very precious to me," she said in a Jan. 3 telephone interview, "from the time he was conceived ... until I gave him permission to go home."

After being in the hospital for two months, Bell requested to spend his last days at home, she said. "His last words to me were, 'Mom, I love you. I'm going home.'"

Michelle Bell created Skipper's Angel Wings shortly after her son was diagnosed with cancer. The organization aims to help raise funds for families who have relatives with cancer. She plans to continue the efforts in memory of her son.

Friends of the family said they will remember Bell's loving spirit.

"He was sweet, he was kind, he was generous, gentle. His smile lit up the room," said Yolanda Delarosa of Eastchester, whose children were friends with Bell.

Delarosa's son, Jonathan, said Bell was like a brother to him.

"He was just an all-around great person," said Jonathan Delarosa, 21, who often cut Bell's hair when he was in the hospital.

Ann Marie DeCairano of Eastchester said she is grateful for the impression Bell made on her son. "He taught my son about giving, about pain and suffering," she said.

"We always did everything together," added her 19-year-old son, Michael, recalling sleepovers where they would pull pranks on each other.

"We would have this contest ...," DeCairano said. "He would draw on you while you were sleeping. And, he always won. He was always undefeated."

Bell kept his humor until the time of his death, Yolanda Delarosa said.

"On the night that he was passing, Jackie kissed him on the forehead and he said, 'Ugh! You spit on me,'" she said and laughed. Jackie Feretti is a family friend. "That we will remember."

Bell was born in Niskayuna, N.Y., on June 20, 1987 to Michele Bell and Nicola Mele. He is survived by his parents, sisters Bianca and Marina Bell and grandmother Barbara Feyl and aunts, uncles and cousins.

Services were held Jan. 3 at Ferncliff Cemetery in Hartsdale. A memorial service will be held at a later date. In lieu of flowers, contributions may be made to Skipper's Angel Wings, Children's Cancer Fund, P.O. Box 266, Eastchester, New York, 10709. For more information about the organization, visit www.skippersangelwings.org.

Reach Hope Salley at hsalley@gannett.com.

What a

WONDERFUL

DIFFERENCE

YOU'VE MADE

IN THE LIVES

OF THE FAMILY

WHO LOVES YOU.

Dear MoM,
 All though we
wont be together
on Christmas DAy,
TRUST ME when I
Tell you I Appreciate
everything and
All you do for
Me I love you
More than words
Can Say.
merry Christmas
Love,
SKIPPER
XOXOXOXOX
12-03

Merry Christmas MoM
I LOVE YOU VERY MUCH
WITH ALL MY HEART
LOVE
SKIPPER

Its a struggle every day just be strong
and theres know way I could pay you
back but my plan is to show you I
understand, I Love you mommy
very much Merry Christmas.
            Love
            NICKY

Friends remember brave youth

Bell kept being the life of the party despite struggle with bone cancer

Hope Salley
Review Press

Caresse VanDoran of Eastchester recalled the good times she shared with her friend Nicola Bell at her high school junior prom about two years ago.

"It was so much fun," the 18-year-old said in a Jan. 5 interview. "We went to the prom together. He was so excited. ... He would have danced to everything."

Speaking slowly, and laughing occasionally, VanDoran talked about the teenager who befriended her four years ago in the ninth grade at Eastchester High School.

She and other teens in the community grieved over Bell, who died last week.

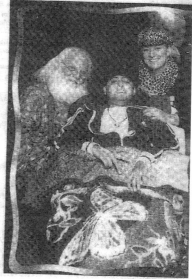

Courtesy of Michele F

Nicola Bell smiles in a photo taken with his mother, Michele, and Santa Claus at the Galleria mall in White Plains a week before his death.

Bell, known both as "Nicky" and "Skipper" to family and friends, died in his Tuckahoe home Dec. 29. He was 18 and had been diagnosed with bone cancer, Ewing's sarcoma, in November 2001.

"He was so sick with cancer, yet you never heard him say 'my life is so unfair,'" VanDoran said. "He was always trying to help his friends. Even when he was struggling really bad and we would come over he would always say 'drive safely.'"

She and other friends held a vigil outside of Bell's home the night he died.

According to Michelyn Ferretti, 17, of Eastchester, Bell had a way of drawing people to him. "He had an aura that made you feel OK when you were around him ... a sparkle in his eye. He was put through a lot of difficult times, but through everything he kind of stayed strong."

She said one of Bell's last large gatherings with his friends was at the VIP Country Club in New Rochelle. His family and friends held a surprise birthday party there for him in June. "He walked in and he was so surprised. He thought he was going to a wedding with his mom," she said and laughed.

Family and friends also held a Christmas party for Bell and took him to the Galleria mall in White Plains a week before his death to take a photograph with Santa Claus.

Many of his friends will remember Bell's sense of humor the most. "He was absolutely hysterical! Up until the very end," VanDoran said.

Bell's mother, Michele, said that was an attribute that made him different. She mentioned his humor in a eulogy at his funeral services at Ferncliff Cemetery in Hartsdale last week. "He had a great off-beat sense of humor that caressed his friends and family ... He was the son who would watch all the comedy films with me and play little jokes on me," Bell said in the eulogy.

"He was always an upbeat kind of person," 18-year-old Mario Aloia of Eastchester said, recalling a trip Bell took with him and other friends to the Bahamas last year during spring break from school.

Bell played a prank on him while he was sleeping. "I took baby powder and threw it on my face while I w sleeping. When I woke up, I was all white ... He just lov to have a good time," Aloia said.

"He was always part of the parties," added anoth friend, Joelle Bonci, 18, of Eastchester. "He liked kinds of music ... he even liked Frank Sinatra."

Those who knew Bell will keep the happy memori in their hearts as they remember a boy who kept a sm on his face, despite his pain and struggles.

VanDoran said Bell taught her a life lesson: "App ciate everything you have ... You can overcome obs cles," she said. "He was truly an amazing person."

Michele Bell plans to continue a nonprofit she start about four years ago called Skipper's Angel Wings raise funds for families who have relatives with cance Skipper is a nickname she gave her son as a baby.

"Hopefully, we'll start more fundraisers in the sprir because it was my passion to help families who we through what I went through. I'm a single mother, ar I lost my home, my job, but never lost my ability to ǵ on and be strong and be there for my son," she said.

A charity basketball game will be held in the Eastc ester High School gymnasium at 7 p.m. March 3 in mer ory of Bell. Proceeds will go to Skipper's Angel Wing Admission is $5 and donations are welcome.

Reach Hope Salley at hsalley@gannett.com.

More information

For information about Skipper's Angel Wings and how to help families caring for relatives with cancer, visit www.skippersangelwings.org.

Nicola Bell, inspiration for Skipper's Angel Wings, dies

Tuckahoe boy, 18, fought brave battle against bone cancer

Ken Valenti
The Journal News

TUCKAHOE — Nicola "Skipper" Bell, the teenager whose fight with cancer led his mother to create an organization to help other children and teenagers battling the disease, has died.

The 18-year-old died at home, which was his wish, said his mother, Michele Bell.

"He was very, very respectful," she said. "He had a vast amount of respect. He never asked for pity.

"He always worried about everybody else, right up until his last breath. And in his last breath, he said, 'Mom, I love you. I'm going home.'"

He died Dec. 29 and services were held yesterday at Ferncliff

Nicola "Skipper" Bell

Cemetery in Hartsdale.

The teen, who went by "Nick" or "Nicky," was well-known throughout Eastchester, his mother said.

"He was extremely loved and admired by the entire community," she said.

At the age of 14, while a freshman at Eastchester High School, he was diagnosed with Ewing's Sarcoma, a form of bone cancer, when doctors found a tumor in his leg.

In 2003, his mother, having lost a job because she needed time to care for her son, began Skipper's Angel Wings.

Through his chemotherapy, blood transfusions and hospital stays, Bell was not alone. His grandmother, Barbara Feyl, drove weekly from Albany to see him, from before the time he was diagnosed.

Bell inspired a closeness among his friends, who stood by him, said family friend Yolanda Delarosa. And a support group of four women — his mother, Delarosa and friends Jackie Perretti and Ann Marie DeCaliano — saw him throughout his ordeal.

"There was nothing we would not have done for that boy," Delarosa said. "Not a thing."

In recent days, his friends lifted his wheelchair into a van to take him to the Galleria mall, Delarosa said. There, he bought a North Face jacket, a cap and sneakers. Always on the forefront of fashion, he owned hundreds of pairs of sneakers, his mother said.

He also had his photograph taken with his mother and Santa Claus.

A Catholic, he was "very, very spiritual," Delarosa said.

He was born June 20, 1987, in Nkayuma, N.Y., to Michele Bell and Nicola Mele.

He is survived by his mother of Tuckahoe and his father, of Albany, two sisters, Bianca-Marina Bell and Isabella Mele, both of Albany; his grandmother, Barbara Feyl, and many aunts, uncles and cousins.

Funeral arrangements were handled by the Westchester Funeral Home in Eastchester.

Donations in his name may be made to Skipper's Angel Wings, Children's Cancer Fund, P.O. Box 266, Eastchester, NY 10708.

"I tell you this kid was the best," Delarosa said. "And he will never be forgotten."

Reach Ken Valenti at kvalenti@thejournalnews.com or 914-696-8255.

Farewell to a brave teen
Family, friends remember Nicola Bell, who lost his fight with cancer. **5**

REFERENCES

American Cancer Society (2015). *Cancer staging.* Retrieved from: http://www.cancer.org/treatment/understandingyourdiagnosis/staging

Darling, J. (2007). The Liddy Shriver Sarcoma Institute. *A different view of sarcoma statistics.* Retrieved from: http://sarcomahelp.org/articles/sarcoma-statistics.html

Elisabeth-Kubler Ross (2005). "On Grief and Grieving" co-written with David Kessler.

Miniño, A. M. (2010). *Mortality among teenagers Aged 12-19 years: United States, 1999-2006.* National Center for Health Statistics. Centers for Disease Control. Retrieved from: http://www.cdc.gov/nchs/products/databriefs/db37.htm

MacMillan Cancer Support (2017). Risk factors and causes of primary bone cancer. http://www.macmillan.org.uk/information-and-support/bone-cancer/diagnosing/causes-and-risk-factors/potential-causes-of-cancer/primary-bone-cancer.html

National Cancer Institute. (2015). *Staging.* Retrieved from: http://www.cancer.gov/about-cancer/diagnosis-staging/staging

University of Texas MD Anderson Cancer Center. (2016). *Ewing's Sarcoma.* Retrieved from: https://www.mdanderson.org/cancer-types/ewings-sarcoma.html

Transitioning Anguish into Empowerment
Dr. Michele Bell Healing Practitioner
www.drmichelebell.com

APA-American Psychological Association
HFA-Hospice Foundation of America
IMPA-International Metaphysical Practitioners Association

This may be the end of *this* story, but it's
not the end of my writing journey.
There are more chapters to come...